A YEAR IN THE GARDEN

365 Inspirational Gardens
and Gardening Tips

Gisela Keil · Jürgen Becker

A YEAR IN THE GARDEN

365 Inspirational Gardens
and Gardening Tips

Prestel
Munich · London · New York

© 2017 Deutsche Verlags-Anstalt, Munich,
a member of Verlagsgruppe Random House GmbH,
Neumarkter Strasse, 81673 Munich,
Germany

© text: Gisela Keil
© images: Jürgen Becker (including Cover)

© for the English edition:
Prestel Verlag,
Munich · London · New York, 2018
A member of Verlagsgruppe Random House GmbH,
Neumarkter Strasse, 81673 Munich,
Germany

Prestel Publishing Ltd.
4, Bloomsbury Place
London WC1A 2QA
UK

Prestel Publishing
900 Broadway, Suite 603
New York, NY, 10003
USA

Frontispiece:
Garden and design: Son Muda Gardens, Majorca (E)
Picture before the appendix:
Garden: Judith Behm-Harding, Majorca (E)

Library of Congress Control Number is available:
British Library Cataloguing-in-Publication Data:
a catalogue record for this book is available from
the British Library.

The Deutsche Nationalbibliothek holds a record for this
publication in the Deutsche Nationalbibliografie; detailed
biographical data can be found under:
http://dnb.ddb.de

Translation: Paul Harrison, Fay Maike Brown (Übersetzerring)

Editorial direction: Dr Thomas Hagen
Copy-editing: Danko Szabó, Jane Michael
Origination: Helio Repro GmbH, Munich
Layout, typesetting & production: Corinna Pickart,
Monika Pitterle
Cover Design: Corinna Pickart
Printing & binding: C&C Joint Printing Co., Ltd.
Paper: Chinese Matt Art

Verlagsgruppe Random House FSC® N001967

Printed in China

ISBN: 978-3-7913-8424-5

Preface

"The garden has become a focal point for influences from all over the world. The little piece of cosmos around our house is slowly turning into a magic workshop with ever more precious possibilities," wrote Karl Foerster, the great plant lover and garden designer, almost a hundred years ago. How right he still is today!

It's true – gardens are a constant temptation to be playful and creative with their huge repertoire of plants, colours, shapes and materials. They're refuges in which children can have their first encounters with nature and gather impressions which will stay with them for a lifetime. These sanctuaries are becoming more and more attractive for an increasing number of young people, especially in cities – and persons of a more advanced age can find fortitude and enjoyment in them too. This isn't surprising, for every garden is a green "magic workshop" – a parallel dimension to our automated and digitalised everyday life where we can come very close to the numerous facets and cycles of nature and sensual reality again. Most people

perceive these paradises of personal freedom and creativity as being gratifying places in which to experience leisure and activity as well as companionship and solitude.

This diary is intended as a companion to the year in the garden and presents seasonal design ideas as well as tips on plants and practical gardening methods in daily instalments.

Splendid images show picturesque gardens of all styles as the seasons change. Of course, there's also space in the diary for daily notes, reminders and observations so that we can record everything the year in the garden gives us.

Gisela Keil and Jürgen Becker wish you a happy gardening year full of wishes which come true, plants which flourish magnificently, ideas which stand the test of time – and weeds which stay away.

Gisela Keil and Jürgen Becker

1 January

The garden year begins gently with a period of rest, a pause for thought, which – in the case of passionate garden lovers – should in no way be equated with doing nothing. In fact, the focus now is on the creative examination of the paradise you've created. It's wonderful, and a charming gesture, whenever winter throws in a few cheerful sunny days to lure us outside. The structure and skeleton of the garden will never be as visible as it is now, nor will its weak points ever manifest themselves more honestly than during these weeks in which the garden is stripped of its leaves. But not only beauty can fire your imagination – shortcomings can too! Now is the time to play through potential improvements, weigh up possibilities and turn your wishes into reality. In short: it's time to make plans, for the gardening year has already begun!

Notes / Birthdays

Who wouldn't like to take a seat in this wintry idyll and let his or her gaze wander off into the distance? But the mere contemplation of a successful design can also make you happy – and inspire creativity.
Garden: Elisabeth Imig and Silke Imig-Gerold (D)

January

2 January

Evergreen cut hedges and other trees and shrubs bordering on streets suffer threefold when road salt is used in winter. If the salt penetrates into the ground with the meltwater, it impairs the absorbance of nutrients, causes cells to die off and damages life in the soil. Before that happens, however, the salt gets to the trees and shrubs in the form of splash water. Dead brown leaf edges and needles, curled brown shoot apexes and permanent poor growth are the result.

· Walls and pedestals help against salting of the soil.
· You can protect the hedges from splash water by fastening heavy-duty plastic film (up to 1.8 metres high) to wooden slats and installing this in front of the hedge throughout the winter.

Notes / Birthdays

_____

_____

_____

_____

The entrance to this garden is enough in itself to arouse your curiosity and make you wonder what kind of paradise awaits the visitor behind the romantically overgrown gate in this beech hedge.
Garden: De Heerenhof (NL)

January

3 January

If plants are in hibernation now, does that mean that they sleep at other times as well? Science's answer is "Yes". Carl von Linné (1707–1778) was one of the first to observe that flowers open and close their blossoms in a day-night rhythm even when they're kept in a dark cellar. Charles Darwin (1809–1882) observed that small plants also let their leaves and stalks hang overnight, and he called this "sleep" too.

Now, researchers at the Finnish Geospatial Research Institute have found out, with the aid of laser scanner technology, that fully grown trees literally "sink into sleep" by as much as 10 cm at night. Then, in the morning, leaves and branches return to their original position.

Notes / Birthdays

Even a garden made to look beautiful in winter with its shrubs, grasses and trees looks numbed and lifeless in the shade. It takes the golden rays of the sun to make it come to life again.
Garden: De Hagenhof (NL)

January

4 January

Make sure at regular intervals that your pond is free of ice in at least one place so that any fish and amphibians hibernating in it get enough oxygen. If the ice covering the pond is closed, don't hack it open, for the sound waves will cause suffering to the pond's inhabitants. Instead, thaw open a hole in the ice and drain off sufficient pond water to create a clear gap between the surface of the water and the sheet of ice.

This layer of air will allow the necessary exchange of gas to take place. Those who wish to do so can then vertically place straw or reed mats tied together into this area to keep it free of ice.

Notes / Birthdays

If the entire pond is frozen and snowy – and not just the edge – clear away some of the snow to allow the light to reach the fish and plants.

5 January

Not all rambler roses are equally winter-hardy. Annual blooming varieties, many of which reward us in autumn with countless rose-hips in small bunches, are regarded as being especially frost-resistant. Examples include 'American Pillar' (crimson pink), 'Chevy Chase' (blood red), *Rosa helenae* (white), 'Polstjärnan' (white), 'Lykkefund' (white, prickle-free), 'Goldfinch' (light yellow). Robust varieties need no protection. Remove frozen shoots in spring. If they freeze back radically, roses sprout strongly after being cut back, enabling them to reach their original height again after two years. In the case of more sensitive varieties, you should pile up soil around the base and loosely wrap reed, coconut or straw mats around them at the bottom.

Notes / Birthdays

Rose-hips are little vitamin bombs. Three normal-size fruits are enough to cover the vitamin C requirements of an adult. The tiny fruits of the rambler roses cannot quite keep up here and are inedible after frost. They still look nice, though, and remain a delicacy for birds.

January

6 January

Snow can be both good and bad for the garden. While providing perfectly insulating protection, it can also cause damage to trees and shrubs.

Powdery snow has the best insulating properties: it's light and is produced in calm weather from fine dry snowflakes. These consist of snow crystals whose shapes differ greatly depending on the temperature at which they formed in the clouds.

Small snowflakes which the wind sticks together to form a firm blanket of snow are dangerous for trees and shrubs – but even more dangerous are large snowflakes which become wet and heavy when temperatures in the soil increase. Both types of snow can lead to breakages, especially in the case of evergreens.

Notes / Birthdays

That snow and hoar frost will cover even Mediterranean sea holly is evident from this example of sea holly *(Eryngium)*. They turn the blossoms, which keep all winter long, into ethereal appetisers.

January

7 January

Spruce and fir tree branches provide an alternative to snow as a natural winter protection.
At the time of the greatest cold, their coat of
needles is still dense and holds off icy winds,
black frosts and strong sunshine. They begin
to shed their needles in spring and let light
through, so that the soil can slowly start to heat
up again. They offer a variety of uses:
· You can lay them over plants and mulch.
· You can insert brushwood twigs into the
  ground at an angle around the plant.
· With fruit trees and climbing trees growing
  on a trellis, fix the branches over one another
  to form scales. This enables the meltwater to
  run off the outside and not into the plant.
Tip: Christmas tree branches can be used for
this purpose too.

Notes / Birthdays

Not only plants need frost protection –
water-filled vessels need it too. You should
empty them before the frost sets in and
cover them up with a film or with boards
so that ice can't break them open.

Garden: Elisabeth Imig and Silke Imig-Gerold (D)

8 January

The number of birds is declining dramatically. Breeding pairs in agricultural regions of the EU, for example, decreased by 57 per cent – equivalent to 300 million birds – between 1980 and 2010. Ever fewer birds are coming into gardens and parks too. Even though feeding the birds there benefits only 10 to 15 different species, most of which are not endangered, it does at least connect the aspect of helping with the joy of experiencing nature. Provide the feed at different places which birds can easily find but which cats can't access. Grain eaters such as tits, finches, bullfinches and sparrows like sunflower seeds and grain mixtures. Eaters of soft feed such as robins, dunnocks, blackbirds, fieldfares and wrens should be given raisins, fruit, oat flakes and bran placed close to the ground and protected against moisture.

Notes / Birthdays

Wreaths and branches from the garden are especially suitable for attractive outdoor decorations, and can also welcome birds with ornamental apples and bird-feeding rings. Grain eaters and soft feed eaters love these fat rings.

Garden: Elisabeth Imig and Silke Imig-Gerold (D)

January

9 January

If your interest in plants is restricted to the blossoms, you often miss some important things. This is also true of the unjustly neglected group of yellow-blooming clematis, such as *Clematis orientalis, Clematis tangutica* and *Clematis serratifolia* and their varieties. All extremely winter-hardy and free of ailments, they grace the garden from June to early spring. Their mainly bell- or balloon-shaped yellow flowers appear until November. These are followed by fluffy silvery seed pods, most of which survive the winter. In spring, cut the plants back to between 20–60 cm – and wait for the fresh splendour to come.
Tip: *Clematis vitalba* has silvery woolly fruits. Be careful, however, for this species needs a lot of space and is extremely hard to keep in check in small and medium-size gardens.

Notes / Birthdays

_____

_____

_____

_____

Hoar frost has iced up the hairy seed pods of this clematis with a silvery glamour. But even without this treatment, they look enchanting all winter long. Afterwards, the hairs function as a flying aid for the seeds.

January

10 January

All is quiet in the fruit and vegetable garden. In addition to winter leeks, there are green cabbages and winter varieties of Brussels sprouts to harvest. These can all withstand temperatures down to -10°C. When temperatures are low, you should cover them up with brushwood or fleece. Green and red cabbages are harvested from the bottom to the top, and light frost gives them a better flavour. Both types of cabbage store sugar with the help of photosynthesis and low temperatures. At below-zero temperatures, the plant's own enzymes are put out of action, as they would otherwise decompose the sugar again. This increases the sugar content of green cabbage and Brussels sprouts and makes them tastier. More recent varieties of green cabbage have a higher sugar content anyway, so you can harvest them all year round, even if there's no frost.

White cabbages still remaining in the bed are varieties of autumn cabbage, which are planted in October and harvested in spring. Unlike green cabbages (at the back), they need a protective covering once temperatures drop below -5°C.

January

11 January

No matter how magical gardens look under a blanket of snow, it must, for reasons of safety, be cleared away from the driveway, house entrance and pavement alongside the plot. In densely populated regions, you often have to shovel the snow into your own front garden for lack of space. This should be taken into account when you plant your front garden. Robust shrubs which have retracted their leaves can withstand snow weighing down on them for a few weeks. Roses and evergreens and other ornamental trees and shrubs, however, can break under the weight. You should also try not to use de-icing salt. It not only damages the plants, but can also harm soft natural stone such as limestone, marble and sandstone in pathways and terrace coverings.

Notes / Birthdays

In winter too, box hedges distinctly trace the outlines of pathways and herbaceous borders. A blanket of snow even gives these evergreen "structuralists" a more striking plasticity than in summer.

Garden and design: Peter Janke (D)

January

12 January

If you're looking for a new and highly decorative element for your garden, you could start planning a knot garden. While herbs and fragrant plants were once preferred for the interlacing ornaments and checkerboard patterns, box is mainly used nowadays (varieties such as 'Suffruticosa' and 'Blauer Heinz'). No matter whether the bed is created with one plant only, with two or three different green tones or with two different colours, begin by sketching the pattern. To transfer it to the bed, use a grid of taut strings in longitudinal and crosswise direction (at a distance of 50 × 50 cm). Then transfer the pattern to the squares, mark it with light-coloured sand and put in the plants along the lines.

Notes / Birthdays

A knot garden has the greatest effect when seen from above. The two colours seen here are produced by box and the red, summergreen Japanese barberry *(Berberis thunbergii* 'Atropurpurea'). *Garden: Kristin Lammerting (D)*

January

13 January

Sphere, cone, figure or hedge – topiarised evergreen trees and shrubs continue to be ordering elements in winter too. They structure gardens, set accents and create separate spaces. This requires a certain amount of care.

- After large snowfalls, topiarised trees and shrubs such as box, yew, holly and cherry laurel must be cleared of snow.
- After cold periods, water them generously on frost-free days when the soil thaws out slightly. Otherwise they risk drying out because they're unable to draw any water from the frozen soil and yet keep on evaporating moisture through their foliage.
- In spots with full sun, use a fleece during the frost period to prevent the sun and the wind from drying them out.

Notes / Birthdays

_____

_____

_____

_____

Evergreen trees and shrubs, such as this beech cone topiarised into a spiral, become shapely sculptures when a downy blanket of snow makes their contours stand out.
Garden: De Hagenhof (NL)

January

14 January

While we use mats to protect the trunks of younger fruit trees from frost (see 30 December), older ones risk having their trunks split from January to March by the combined effects of frost and sun. What can happen is that the trunk heats up on the south side but stays covered in hoar frost on the north side. This can lead to a temperature difference of up to 20°C within the trunk. The fatter the trunk, the greater the risk that this temperature gradient will break open the bark. Protective measures include painting the trunk white up to the crown in order to reflect the heat, or leaning wooden planks against the south side of the trunks for as long as the intense frost continues. Before carrying out these measures, you should remove any pasting rings which may be attached (see 30 September).

Notes / Birthdays

In the informality of country house gardens, high trees remind us even in winter what a restful feeling it is to sit in their shade in summer.
Garden: Heiderose Birkenstock (D)

January

15 January

Walls in the garden should provide protection from intruders, noise and prying eyes. Aside from these useful functions, however, they also provide opportunities for a wide range of designs. Let your imagination run wild!
· A rose arch with a bench in front of the wall makes a romantic bower.
· Climbing plants integrate the walls into the green of the garden and make it seem larger.
· Trellises structure walls in an extremely attractive way. With a mirror behind them, they even form illusionistic windows and arches.
Walls can also be used for:
· wall fountains and water features
· plant racks and reliefs
· lean-to greenhouses and work tables
· espalier fruit in sunny spots.

Notes / Birthdays

_____

_____

_____

_____

In the form of a blind arch, this niche interrupts the course of the wall and provides a place to leave garden ornaments and any utensils you may need in the sitting area.
Garden: private garden, Majorca (E)

January

16 January

If you have an oriental garden, now is the time to walk around it with a watchful eye – for this is when popular trees used in this style begin to reveal typical signs of damage.

Ornamental cherries and other frost-sensitive trees and shrubs can be damaged by frost splitting the trunk (see 14 January). If there's already a split in the bark, wrap string tightly round the trunk on a frost-free day and smear the split with tree wax or another substance designed to close the wound.

Maples and other deciduous or berry trees can easily be diagnosed for coral spot while the leaves are bare. Red spots on dead shoots are tell-tale signs of this fungus. Cut the shoots back into the healthy wood (to a depth of at least 20 cm) and remove them. Don't put them on the compost heap!

Notes / Birthdays

The stillness of winter underlines the meditative power of oriental gardens. As their design is characterised by trees, shrubs and stones, they don't look empty at this time of the year either.

Garten and design: Reinhold Borsch (D)

January

17 January

How can snowflakes, which float down to earth as light as a feather, break thick branches? The answer lies in the variable weight of snow. In cold weather, the snow that falls is dry powder snow, which can weigh about 100 kg per cubic metre. Higher temperatures, by contrast, produce wet, large-flaked snow, a cubic metre of which can weigh up to 200 kg. Snow tends to remain lying on evergreen trees and shrubs such as holly, rhododendron, laurel cherry, box and conifers in much larger quantities than on bare trees. This is why you should shake off the snow after strong snowfall. To do this, beat against the trunks from below using a broom. Never beat against the branches as this would only increase the pressure. Also, shake the trees and shrubs carefully as frosty wood breaks easily.

Notes / Birthdays

In oriental gardens, the Japanese maple *(Acer palmatum)* has little to fear from blankets of wet snow. However, many evergreen grasses, especially bamboo, are pushed apart or bent more easily the larger they are.
Garden and design: Reinhold Borsch (D)

January

18 January

Bamboo is one of the evergreen grasses and should, like them, be protected from snow, sun, wind and – last but not least – drought. Water it on frost-free days, spread a 20-cm-high layer of mulch around the base, tie it together as a measure against falling snow, or use mats or fleece to protect it. *Fargesia murielae* and its varieties (which form clusters) and stoloniferous species of *Phyllostachys* (which have to be planted with a rhizome barrier) are winter-hardy down to -25°C. There's no need to worry if leaves are shed. Don't remove blades without leaves, as new leaves will sprout there in spring. The roots, however, should be prevented from drought. The protective mats can be removed on a dull day in March. The same is true for dead blades.

Notes / Birthdays

In contrast to bamboo, Japanese Silver Grass *(Miscanthus),* whose blades look so charming in winter, is not an evergreen. It can unfold its beauty freely in regions with little snow and rain, but in other areas should be tied together to form a tuft.

Garden: Anja and Piet Oudolf, design: Piet Oudolf (NL)

January

19 January

Plants growing close to the house need particular attention in winter. As a general rule, pick a spot close to the house, where plants are protected from cold, wind and sunlight. On the other hand, you should take the following into account:

- Regardless of whether they're roses, pears, peaches or apricots, trees and shrubs growing on the wall trellis of a house must be watered on frost-free days in winter and shaded using brushwood, sacking or reed mats in places in full sun from January onwards.
- To ensure that trees and shrubs growing close to the house aren't damaged by roof avalanches, you should construct an overhanging roof to catch the masses of falling snow.
- Care should be taken when moving about close to the house to avoid injury from falling icicles.

This voluminous frost-resistant concrete vessel with its filling of orpine *(Sedum telephium)* benefits from the sheltered spot close to the house.
Garden: Elisabeth Imig and Silke Imig-Gerold (D)

January

20 January

If you want to enrich your garden by adding a new ornamental element, you'll find further inspiration alongside the decorative pebble pathways in the photo on the right. How about an evergreen garden sofa? The brick sitting area shouldn't be too large, so that enough room remains for box "upholstery" to spread behind it and at the sides. When planting the sitting area, we recommend using a brick-built or ready-made planting box equipped with water drainage holes in which to plant heath pearlwort *(Sagina subulata)*.

This piece of outdoor furniture becomes a fragrant bench if blossomless chamomile *(Chamaemelum nobile* 'Treneague') or thyme invite you to rest on the seat instead.

Looking at this garden sofa is just as nice as sitting on it. The artful pebble mosaic design of the pathways is continued in the sofa.
Garden: Kristin Lammerting (D)

January

21 January

Fruit trees will age prematurely and not bear very much fruit if they aren't cut back. Apple and pear trees should be pruned on a sunny, frost-free day.

Whether the trees are to be cut back in order to train, conserve or rejuvenate them depends on their age and condition. Anyone who wishes to learn more about tree-cutting should attend one of the courses provided by many gardening associations at this time of the year. The remains of any fruit still hanging from apple, pear and plum trees should be removed now at the latest. Their wizened surfaces are often infected by the light-coloured spore cushions of the monilia fungus. Keep them away from the compost heap to ensure that they don't cause new infections.

Notes / Birthdays

Don't cut back trees and shrubs at sub-zero temperatures. At temperatures below -5°C, the wood is so brittle that deep splits can form when you prune them.

Garden: Heiderose Birkenstock (D)

22 January

If nothing needs to be planted, maintained or harvested, that leaves plenty of time to be creative and make new plans. Fences and garden gates are more clearly visible now that they're no longer covered in green, so this is a good time to check their appearance and condition. Maybe only a few places or hinges are in need of repair. A new coat of paint is often all that's needed to make the garden entrance and fencing attractive again. On the other hand, a beautiful and original gate is a promising calling card for the garden and its owners. Now is the time to look for elaborate models and the necessary craftsmen – or perhaps even attend a welding course for metalworking.

Notes / Birthdays

With its artfully wrought floral motifs, this iron gate shows that this is the entrance to a realm in which plants have a special status.
Garden: Waltham Place (GB)

January

23 January

A good deal of thought often goes into designing herbaceous borders close to terraces and sitting areas. Towards the back, however, the garden can become dull and boring. The time has now come to plan ways to optimise its design. In this case, plants and objects which look good from a distance are popular for the bottom of the garden. The following are suitable here:

- Plants with large blossoms in white or luminous shades (such as hydrangeas)
- Small-flowered plants in white, pastel or luminous shades (such as *Gaura lindheimeri)*, which are, however, planted over a large area
- Ornamental foliage plants with silvery, white- or yellowish-green leaves (such as *Brunnera macrophylla* 'Jack Frost')
- Large and tall garden objects covering a relatively large area (such as amphorae and benches) or trellises in blue, white or red.

Notes / Birthdays

The dark shapes of two thick yew cylinders in the background suffice as a calm counterpoint to the glistening and wildly branched detail all around.
Garden: Anja and Piet Oudolf,
design: Piet Oudolf (NL)

January

24 January

The way in which the Dutch garden designer Piet Oudolf presented the grasses in the world-famous circular flower bed in his garden was truly brilliant. Anyone who feels inspired by it should bear in mind that, even in a scaled-down version, this formal garden element will need a lot of space around it if it's to have the desired effect.

The plants rest on an elevated circular bed on a base formed by alternating sections made of brick and yew. The centre is dominated by Japanese Silver Grass *(Miscanthus sinensis* 'Malepartus'), which is enclosed all round by the not particularly sturdy palm sedge *(Carex muskingumensis).*

Notes / Birthdays

Thanks to its size and prominent position, Japanese Silver Grass in winter resembles icy creatures marching up. Despite the freestyle way in which it has been planted here, the exact frame of the circular flower bed lends it a formal character.
Garden: Anja and Piet Oudolf,
design: Piet Oudolf (NL)

January

25 January

If you would like to have a highly attractive and yet cosy seat reminiscent of a bower, this example of a circular trellis hedge may well fascinate you. In a circle with a diameter of 6 metres, the owners of the garden inserted eight T-profiles, each 3.5 metres long, into concrete foundations at regular intervals to a depth of 60 cm. After the concrete had dried, a specialist welded on horizontal steel rods at a height of 2 and 2.5 metres to connect the supports and form a circular framework, as well as eight struts for the roof. To increase stability, S-shaped metal sections were soldered on as angle brackets. Only then were the common limes (*Tilia × vulgaris* 'Pallida') – purchased as pre-cultivated trellis trees – planted in it.

Notes / Birthdays

_____

_____

_____

_____

Surrounding the base of this circular bed and trellis hedge is a double row of box hedge, which lends it a distinctive beauty in winter too. In January, it's high time to remove all the annual shoots. The new shoots are then drawn along the trellis to the roof.
Garden: De Heerenhof (NL)

26 January

"What could I still improve and redesign in my garden?" is a question many people ask themselves in these quiet times. You can often achieve great effects with little effort by using colour – an emotional conveyor of moods characterising the atmosphere in the garden. Colour can also be used to set contrasting accents or connect elements harmoniously. The latter has succeeded perfectly in the example on the right, where the reddish-purple back wall of the pergola takes up basic tones of the bricks, the herbaceous borders and even the clematis on the pergola. Chromatic harmony of this kind between plants and garden features leads to balanced and contemplative garden scenarios.

Notes / Birthdays

The supports of a pergola are often made of different materials than the roof. Here, the side walls and rear wall are also made of brickwork, providing a special feel-good atmosphere and turning the bench into an elegant feature of this urban garden.
Design: Brigitte Röde (D)

27 January

Many shrubs (like asters, astilbes, lady's mantle, peonies, phlox or violets) are cold-germination plants that require temperatures around freezing point in order to germinate. You should do the sowing now at the latest.

- Keep the seeds indoors at 15–18°C for about 3–4 weeks to make them swell.
- Keep the sowing pans at about 10°C for a week.
- Only then are they taken outside on a frost-free day to a shady sheltered place. When the first cotyledons appear after 4–8 weeks, continue to cultivate the seeds in a light and frost-free place. Cold-germination plants germinate irregularly and can even take two years at times!

Tip: when you buy seeds of cold-germination plants, ask whether they've been pretreated to allow them to be sown directly in spring.

Notes / Birthdays

Thick downy blankets of snow are no problem for wicker baskets or a winterproof bench, or even for seed pans and the seeds of cold-germination plants kept on them.

Garden and design: Peter Janke (D)

January

28 January

Minimalist gardens are becoming more and more popular as an equivalent to modern cubist architecture – and are usually easy to maintain into the bargain. Their typical characteristics are as follows:

- Reduction to the essential – that is to say, few materials, plants and accessories
- A structure characterised by clear shapes
- Preference is given to plants with a pronounced language of forms, such as grasses, topiarised evergreen trees and shrubs, ground covers and bamboo.
- Instead of blossoms and colours, viewers are offered growth forms, leaf structures and textures.
- Even when geometrical forms are dominant, this style of garden – unlike classical formal gardens – dispenses with a classical structure around a principal axis.

Notes / Birthdays

In this minimalist garden, seat, pergola, pathway and beds have been consistently designed with straight lines and right angles. Even the elevated bed and the mobile outdoor kitchen fit into the concept.

Garden: Landesgartenschau Zülpich, design: GartenLandschaft Berg (D)

January

29 January

Something that winter shows quite distinctly but which never ceases to cause uncertainty in gardening circles is the difference between evergreen, wintergreen and summergreen.

- Evergreens are plants whose leaves or needles stay green and remain suspended from the twig for at least two years, so that the plants are constantly green. This applies in particular to trees and shrubs, with the conifers retaining their needles for a very long time (up to 11 years for firs and 5 years for pines).
- Plants are said to be wintergreen if they go through the winter with green foliage. When the new shoots sprout in spring, however, the foliage is usually shed or becomes unattractive. Shrubs are the main representatives here.
- Summergreen is a synonym for "deciduous" and applies to trees and shrubs.

Notes / Birthdays

Only winter is able to present the differing effects of evergreen and deciduous trees and shrubs so picturesquely. Here, we see a rhythmical hedge backdrop of yews between deciduous trees and shrubs covered in hoar frost.

Garden: Anja and Piet Oudolf,
design: Piet Oudolf (NL)

January

30 January

Wood ash from a tile stove should only be spread to a limited extent in the garden – if at all. Its proportion of burnt lime (calcium oxide) of up to 45 per cent can lead to burned leaves and damage life in the soil. Wood ash should never be used
- in fruit and vegetable gardens, as firewood and its ash can contain a high level of heavy metals
- under rhododendrons, hydrangeas or camellias, as they're unable to cope with the high pH value of 11–13
- for compost.

And if you still don't want to do without it, use only ash from untreated wood and spread it in very small quantities. The best place to do this is on the lawn.

Notes / Birthdays

To ensure that shrubs survive the winter as splendidly as those seen here, they should be treated with fertiliser according to their needs after being cut back in March. Heavy feeders (such as larkspur) get a second helping of fertiliser after the blossom.
Garden: Anja and Piet Oudolf, design: Piet Oudolf (NL)

January

31 January

The colours of tree bark shine through clearly from the pallet of melancholy winter tones. When choosing trees, it's worth taking the regional snowfall into account.

Whereas shoots that are red (such as *Cornus alba* 'Sibirica', *Acer palmatum* 'SangoKaku', *Berberis thunbergii* 'Red Chief'), yellow (such as *Cornus sericea* subsp *sericea* 'Flaviramea', *Acer rufinerve* 'Winter Gold') or green (such as *Acer capillipes, Kerria japonica, Jasminum nudiflorum)* contrast refreshingly with snowy scenarios, white and silvery-grey bark have a greater effect in a snow-free, brownish-green environment.

Tip: a background of evergreen trees and shrubs or an evergreen ground cover (such as ivy or pachysandra) also make colourful shoots stand out more.

Notes / Birthdays

Thanks to their tolerance to pruning, topiarised common beeches *(Fagus sylvatica)* and English yews *(Taxus baccata)* can enrich the winter and turn the colourful bioclimatic architecture of walls and gateways into a tunnel of beech.

Garden: Anja and Piet Oudolf, design: Piet Oudolf (NL)

January

1 February

As long as trees are still bare, their shape can be corrected well with pruning. If a thicker branch needs to be removed in the process, this should be done in three steps:
- Cut a relief notch into the branch from below about 50 cm in front of the intended cutting point.
- Cut through the branch from above about 5 cm from the relief notch. It will fall to the ground under its own weight.
- Finally, the branch stump is removed by cutting at the branch collar, at a slight slant away from the trunk of the tree. The branch collar is the swollen bulge at the base of older branches. Its tissues are capable of regenerating and will later form a scar tissue covering the wound, as well as new shoots.

Notes / Birthdays

Older trees don't always abide by garden boundaries, so thick or rotten branches must occasionally be removed.
Garden: Heiderose Birkenstock (D)

February

2 February

Seeds are capable of germination for varying lengths of time, although they can certainly be stored for two years. Before going to the effort of sowing, check older packets of seeds. If their use-by date isn't printed on the package, a germination test is recommendable. To do this, place a damp piece of kitchen towel on a plate and count out 50 seeds onto it. So that no moisture can escape, the plate should be covered with cling film and placed in a bright place but out of direct sunlight at 20°C. After several days, count the number of seeds which have germinated. If less than half have done so, sowing will not be worthwhile.

Notes / Birthdays

From Candlemas (2 February) onwards, day length increases by 3–4 minutes per day. Even though sunny days seem brighter, the amount of light is still too low to begin sowing seeds on the windowsill

Garden: De Hagenhof (NL)

February

3 February

The name of the picturesque evergreen shrub now beginning to blossom fragrantly with shiny, dark green fan-shaped flowers is not very flattering. Stinking hellebore *(Helleborus foetidus)* is its official name, although the leaves don't stink, but rather give off a musky odour when crushed between the fingers. Those who prize its decorative evergreen foliage call it bear's foot. Like all *Helleborus*, it's extremely poisonous, but also very easy to care for, as it's a native perennial. It likes poor, chalky soil and slight shade, and seeds itself abundantly in spots which fit its requirements. The only care required is after blossoming, when all the faded flowers should be removed back to the upper-most pair of leaves.

Notes / Birthdays

The evergreen stinking hellbore *(Helleborus foetidus,* see also 24 February) is not to be beaten by snow and ice. Its bell-shaped, sometimes red-edged blossoms appear from February to April and are an extremely popular and important early source of food for bumble-bees and wild bees.

February

4 February

Forced spring blossoms such as Christmas roses, primroses, crocuses, dwarf narcissi, snow-drops, tulips and hyacinths are now waiting in nurseries and garden centres to spread spring-time flair in and around the house. But coming from greenhouses, they're unaccustomed to cold, frosty nights and heavy layers of snow. At night-time, they should therefore be brought into the house or covered with a layer of fleece in the garage. A cool, bright place at about 10°C is ideal for them – certainly not room temperature. Those who nevertheless want to use them as room decoration should at least put them in a cool place at night. Don't throw faded plants away; they can be planted in the garden from March.

Notes / Birthdays

You can get hold of exquisite treasures in garden centres, for example *Helleborus × ericsmithii* (with reddish brown leaves), *Cyclamen coum*, varieties of *Galanthus nivalis*, Helleborus foetidus and filled varieties of Helleborus.
Garden and design: Peter Janke (D)

February

M. PLANCK INST.
OBST

5 February

Now is the time to prune pome fruit trees (apple, pear). Stone fruit (cherry, damson, peach, apricot, plums etc.), on the other hand, should be pruned during or after harvesting. Cutting back apple and pears trees is usually done in January (see 21 January).
In extremely cold regions, however, it's better to wait until the end of February. The reason is that from the end of January onwards, sap starts flowing back into the trees and they slowly begin to sprout again. Early pruning particularly encourages growth, forcing trees which have been cut back in good time to sprout sooner and subsequently suffer more from late frost damage than trees which are pruned later.

Notes / Birthdays

In rural gardens with a variety of fruit trees, pruning shears and saws are now in action on a large scale.

February

6 February

An apple screen hedge such as this can be planted even in decorative gardens. It's ideal alongside a path, as a partition or at the garden boundary, blends in well with small gardens and is easier to care for and harvest, not just for the elderly. Before beginning, it's best to ask at a tree nursery for precise information on suitable varieties and the required varieties for fertilisation. Also, it's imperative that the trees are grafted onto a slow-growing base. First, the trellis must be erected. Point foundations of concrete should be created at intervals of 2 metres, and wooden or metal posts of the desired height placed into them. Fixed wires should be stretched between the posts at horizontal intervals of 50 cm. The trees are then planted in the middle between the posts and their branches led along the tiered wires.

Notes / Birthdays

Such an attractive screen hedge of apple trees is sure to motivate some decorative gardeners not to miss the taste of self-harvested fruit.

Garden: Nina Balthau (B)

February

7 February

When there's already an old tree at the heart of the garden, and a sociable meeting place for eating and celebrating together is at the top of your wish-list, why not combine the two? The solution on the right requires a standard fruit tree whose roots are resistant to the extra load, such as broad-crowned varieties of apple and ornamental apple *(Malus)* or of cherry and ornamental cherry *(Prunus)*. As the seating area is permanently installed, it must withstand all weather conditions. The solidly built base therefore has a deep ground foundation, while the table top and seating surfaces are made of thick hardwood planks. It's less burdensome for the tree roots when only the table has a solidly built base and is then combined with mobile benches or chairs.

Notes / Birthdays

The shade provider is included in this picturesque seating area, and allows visitors to experience the changing seasons close up with growing leaves, blossoms and fruits.
Garden: De Hagenhof (NL)

February

8 February

Migratory birds return at the end of this month. They occupy their territories and, like non-migratory birds, search for suitable breeding grounds. Nest boxes and nest holes should be cleaned and mounted by then.

The right spot for a bird home is shady and faces south-east or east. In large gardens, it's best to hang several boxes with different-size entrance holes for various types of birds. They should be installed 15–30 metres apart (territories!) and tilted slightly forward so that water cannot run in, but instead drips off. "Nest boxes with marten protection" are ideal – and can be found on the Internet. By the way, birds don't need perches. At most, these help their predators.

Notes / Birthdays

Even in winter, watering cans and bird cages stand almost symbolically for what gardens can mean: duty and care, but also taking delight in something special and enjoyment.

Garden: Heiderose Birkenstock (D)

February

9 February

As redcurrants and gooseberries sprout and blossom very early, they should already be pruned now on frost-free days.

- For redcurrant and whitecurrant shrubs, the old dark-coloured main shoots should be cut back, so that a maximum of 8–10 shoots remain. From there, all the side shoots are removed up to 30 cm above ground level. The remaining side shoots are shortened to 3–5 buds.
- For gooseberries, the framework of the shrubs should be built on 8–10 main shoots. Gooseberries tend to form a lot of side shoots and become too dense. They should therefore be thinned out. Additionally, the leader branches should be shortened slightly; the remaining side shoots to just 3–7 eyes.

Notes / Birthdays

Even rusty, discarded garden tools are too good to be thrown away. This is an original example of upcycling as elements of a fence around a farm garden.
Garden: Susanne Paus, Peter Zweil (D)

February

10 February

Cutting back clematis correctly is simple – as long as you know which pruning groups your plants belong to.

- Group 1: includes the spring bloomers, such as *Clematis alpina, Cl. macropetala* and *Cl. montana* with its numerous varieties. They shouldn't be pruned, but can be thinned out as necessary if required.
- Group 2: the large-blossomed hybrids which bloom in late spring and again in late summer should be pruned back now to between a third and a half of their size.
- Group 3: comprises summer and autumn bloomers. This includes large-blossomed hybrids, *Clematis viticella, Cl. orientalis, Cl. tangutica, Cl. texensis* and *Cl. serratifolia,* all of which have lots of varieties. Their shoots are cut back to a length of 30–50 cm.

Notes / Birthdays

The thick and tangled rose tendrils on this pergola mean lots of time-consuming pruning for gardeners. With its thin shoots, clematis, on the other hand, can be cut back in no time.
Garden: De Heerenhof (NL)

February

11 February

When lawns and flower beds transform into craterous landscapes, the first step is to identify the perpetrator. If the saboteur is a mole, you cannot catch it in a trap, but only scare it off, as moles are protected. Voles are a different matter. Here are some helpful criteria to differentiate the two when searching for evidence.

· Mole tunnels are horizontally oval and full of roots hanging down, as the insect eaters don't nibble on them. To scare them off, spray a piece of cotton wool with old perfume and place it in the tunnel.

· The tunnels of the plant-eating voles are vertically oval and free of roots inside. If you remove the heaps of earth and open up the entrance, the vole will fill it up again very quickly.

Notes / Birthdays

The picturesque contrast between tall, delicate deciduous trees and the dark, closed shapes of yew sculptures distracts from the unattractive bumps beneath them in the lawn.
Garden: De Wiersse (NL)

February

12 February

Alongside early crocuses and snowdrops, winter aconites *(Eranthis hyemalis)* in particular are a feast for the eyes and the first treat for bees and bumble-bees in February. As it can take a number of years for them to seed themselves and spread like a carpet, some people hesitate to bring them into the garden.

A faster way is to plant them, which you can do now. Purchase pre-cultivated plants and use them as outdoor decoration. On frosty nights, they need to be covered with newspaper, fleece or bubble wrap. After they've faded, they should be planted into gaps. The following year, they then bloom more reliably than when the bulbs are planted in autumn. Attractive varieties: 'Schwefelglanz' (cream white), 'Plena', 'Noel Ayers' (filled), 'Aurantiaca', 'Pauline' (light apricot).

Notes / Birthdays

Winter aconites are well suited to running wild in meadows and for planting under or in front of shrubs, roses and wooded areas. The foliage retracts after the seeds have formed in May, so they disturb neither summer blossoms nor mowing.

February

13 February

"If I could go back twenty years, I would plant a grove of these two Asians. And now I would have plenty of tall shrubs to choose from and would not need to be so stingy when friends ask for a branch," wrote Vita Sackville-West. She was referring to the slow growth of witch hazel, and particularly of Chinese witch hazel *(Hamamelis mollis)* and Japanese witch hazel *(Hamamelis japonica),* which bloom from January, depending on their location and the climate. Today, it's the large-blossomed and thickly flowered hybrids *(Hamamelis × intermedia)* that are usually planted, of which there are yellow, orange, red and copper-brown varieties. The tassel-shaped flowers are most effective against a house wall or in front of dark-coloured evergreen shrubs.

Notes / Birthdays

Even when it's extremely cold, the delicately fragranced ribbon-shaped witch hazel flowers *(Hamamelis × intermedia)* don't freeze. They roll up and unfold again on warmer days. The blossoms usually last for three to four weeks.

February

14 February

Those who have been given a bouquet of flowers for Valentine's Day can sustain the gift a little longer with a few tricks.

- Narcissi exude a slimy sap from their stems when cut, which can make other flowers wilt quickly. Before they're placed in a vase with other flowers, special preparation is required (see 14 May).
- Tulip stalks continue to grow longer in vases. To prevent this growth and also stop the flowers from opening and falling off too soon, pierce each stem below the flower with a needle and only fill the vase 5–8 cm deep with water.
- Christmas roses stay fresh for longer in vases and decorations if you cut upwards into their stems from the bottom.

Notes / Birthdays

For plant lovers, the first snowdrop blooming on Valentine's Day can be the best present. Seen here is the filled variety *Galanthus nivalis* 'Hippolyta' with long outer petals and heart-shaped green markings on the inner petals.

February

15 February

When the days get shorter in autumn, the cell sap of plants thickens. The more sugar and salt are dissolved in it, the more frost-tolerant the cells become. From about the middle of January, this effect decreases and the roots begin to take in more water again. Although an apple bud, for example, can survive -50°C in December, it will freeze at the end of March at just -10°C, and cannot even tolerate -4°C shortly before opening. Therefore, a warm period in February means that a subsequent cold spell can do great damage.

Notes / Birthdays

The light already gives a foretaste of spring. But the pool in this modern formal garden is still covered, and the apple trees with their multitude of vertical suckers clearly still need pruning.
Garden: De Heerenhof (NL)

February

16 February

After the long drabness of winter, it's entirely understandable if the people begin to yearn for a southern way of life. Why not immerse the terrace in Mediterranean flair and transform it into a little holiday paradise? Simply replace the sunshade and awning with a planted pergola – beneath which decorative walls and floor coverings of natural stone or gravel provide the open-air home with a permanent framework. Uniform paving or tiling gains a certain something when you remove individual stones or tiles and replace them with fanciful mosaics.

And then it depends on the right choice of furniture, plants and containers to transform the terrace into a spot for southern-style enjoyment of life.

Notes / Birthdays

No Mediterranean *dolce vita* is complete without a large table at which to eat and celebrate together. An expansive table with plenty of seating is at the heart of the southern way of life.
Design: Maria Sagreras, Viveros Pou Nou (E)

February

17 February

When planning, who wouldn't be interested in giving their garden a new, attractive element, without needing to carry out a far-reaching redesign? In that case, it's worth upgrading a small, hitherto neglected niche. Useful and also refreshing, water always has a symbolic meaning as a source of life. A water supply for a fountain is particularly easy to install near the house – in a terrace wall, for example, or in the facade of the house, on the garage wall or on the privacy wall between terraced houses. Once the technology has been installed, you should choose the waterspout and basin carefully, as they influence the style and atmosphere – and also often define the use of the water feature.

In this garden on Majorca, the stairway is cleverly used for a wall fountain and is also planted with a gorgeous red bougainvillea.
Garden: Judith Behm-Harding (E)

February

18 February

In the main pruning phase, some gardeners wonder about trees "bleeding". Like people and animals (with arteries and veins), trees also have two circulatory systems. In one (xylem), water and nutrients are transported upwards from the roots, while in the other (phloem), compounds produced in the leaves during photosynthesis are sent downwards to where they're required. In the rest period between October and February, the sap hardly flows when trees are pruned. There's also very little sap lost in the vegetation period between May and September. These periods are therefore favourable for cutting back. The sap pressure is greatest before budding between the middle of March and May. It's still unclear, however, whether or how much "bleeding" actually damages trees.

Notes / Birthdays

A Japanese maple *(Acer palmatum)* grows attractively even without pruning. Even so, maples, walnut trees, grapevines, birch trees, robinia and tulip trees should be cut back very early, as they "bleed" much more than other trees.
Garden: Japanese Garden Bayer Leverkusen (D)

February

19 February

Those who would like to add a popular element to a Far Eastern garden in the new garden year could perhaps choose an arch bridge.

These designs, which come from the Chinese culture, are called *soribashi*. Like all Asian elements, the bridges have not only a practical side, but also a symbolic meaning as the connection between two worlds. In China and Japan, boating has always been popular. And when a *soribashi* is viewed from the water or the land, the arch's reflection in the water completes it to form a round moon. But an arch bridge can also lead over a "river" of gravel or pebbles, even without a stream or pond.

Notes / Birthdays

The subtle brown-red of this arch bridge even blends in well with the winter world. Red-painted bridges and gateways in Far Eastern gardens are supposed to constantly spread a cheerful atmosphere.
Garden: Japanese Garden Bayer Leverkusen (D)

February

20 February

A paradise for plants can also be created in a small space if the design includes a vertical axis. Raised beds and a pergola make this possible in the example on the right. The fact that the small garden area still seems generous despite the variety of plants is also thanks to other good solutions:

- Clear surfaces (gravel paths and the raised bed edges of corten steel) create a peaceful counterpart to the varied planting.
- The uniform earthy tones of all elements don't distract from the structure and the plants.
- The classic concept of a square of flower beds with a tall element in the centre is modified. Here, a space-saving fountain replaces the usual objects and gives the scene an airy feel.

You can never collect enough ideas for garden planning. The fountain in the centre of this garden, which is divided into four parts, enriches the area both visually with an ethereal height element and acoustically through the babbling sound of water.

Design: Planorama (D)

February

21 February

Sunshades are essential for balconies and terraces. If there isn't much space, it's doubly important to not clutter up the limited space. Also, those who don't wish to be constantly shifting the parasol in summer should perhaps consider an awning, especially since this also shields from unwanted glances from above. There are three basic types:

- The canopy and frame of full-cassette retractable awnings can be pulled back into a closed cover.
- Semi-cassette retractable awnings are open at the bottom, while the canopy and roller are protected from above by a roof.
- Open awnings have no protection and are best suited for use under eaves.

Notes / Birthdays

Terraces should always suit the architecture. Taking the place of the classic wall fountain is a modular ensemble of pool and water wall, into which the necessary technology is installed.
Design: Brigitte Röde (D)

February

22 February

If lesser celandine *(Ranunculus ficaria)* suddenly starts sprawling over the garden, there's no need to despair. The shiny leaves, which are rich in vitamin C, can be picked for use in salads, quark dishes, herb dips or smoothies until the gold-yellow flowers open. As soon as they begin to taste bitter, however, and at the latest when the plants begin to bloom, the little ground covering plants must be banned from the kitchen – as the level of poisonous protoanemonin has then risen to the point that eating the leaves will upset the stomach. Even when the plants' leaves are rampant over large areas, they don't necessarily need to be weeded out. In May or June at the latest, the uninvited guest leaves the flower beds and retreats to its root tubers until the following year.

Notes / Birthdays

The lesser celandine begins depositing increased quantities of toxic substances when it blossoms, and is then no longer edible. It does, however, still have plenty to offer bumble-bees and bees, which it attracts as if by magic with its radiant yellow leaves.

February

23 February

Evergreen shrubs need protection from evaporation and drying sunshine during black frosts and sunny days, especially now (see also 13 January). They've also developed techniques of their own to protect themselves and survive the winter undamaged. The rhododendron is a good example of this. By letting leaves droop and rolling them up, they reduce the size of their leaves, thus minimising the level of evaporation. As soon as they're no longer able to obtain water from the frozen ground, the water pressure in the leaves sinks and they begin to curl up. At the same time, the lack of water leads to an increase in certain substances in the sap which act as an antifreeze. You can help the plants by watering them on frost-free days.

Notes / Birthdays

In mild regions, *Mahonia* × *media* 'Winter Sun' sometimes blooms in November, otherwise from January to April. In cold regions, this evergreen solitary bush, which grows to a height of 1.5–2.5 metres, needs protection to prevent winter sun and frost from damaging the leaves.

February

24 February

Gall mites can cause the needles of conifers to turn brown and fall off, and lead to deformities in the shoots of deciduous trees and ornamental shrubs. Their impact on berry bushes, however, is far worse: blackcurrants in particular, but also redcurrants and whitecurrants, raspberries and blackberries can be affected. The swollen, balloon-like buds can be easily spotted before the leaves appear. Each bud can contain up to 30,000 mites and 20,000 eggs. From March onwards, the mites leave their home and colonise new buds, where they multiply rapidly. The affected fruits don't ripen, and can also carry viruses. Remove the round buds now, and cut back the shoots in cases of heavy infestations. Alternatively, plant mite-resistant varieties.

Notes / Birthdays

Although work in the garden is gradually picking up again, take your time to enjoy the first flowers of spring. Peeking out of the ground here are winter aconite, snowdrops and *Helleborus foetidus*.
Garden and design: Peter Janke (D)

February

25 February

During long winters, wild animals often venture into rural gardens. If tracks lead into your garden, you should examine beds with winter vegetables and the bark of young trees, which hungry hares often nibble on. Protect the vegetables by covering them with fleece, and the tree trunks by sheathing them in wire mesh or special plastic spirals.

Deer, on the other hand, prefer the shoots of young trees or berry bushes, which can be made less appealing to animals by painting them with a chilli paste (mix chilli powder into oil), or hanging a nylon stocking filled with dog hairs in them.

Notes / Birthdays

Nature and forest gardens appear particularly harmonious if their elements have a natural flair, such as this bark mulch path. The fact that the pillars and the vase don't seem out of place here is thanks to their earthy tones.
Garden and design: Peter Janke (D)

February

26 February

Even the most attractive seating group can seem forlorn on large terraces if the design potential of these outdoor seating areas isn't used. Give the terrace a protective frame. For this, you can use surrounding walls, cut hedges, balustrades, flower beds, individual shrubs, trellis fences and pergolas, as well as potted plants which border the edge of the terrace in individual groups and also protect from unwanted glances and wind. These elements don't need to form a uniform or hermetic seal around the terrace.

Often, a few hints are enough to give an impression of comfort and safety – and to keep away the cold rising from the ground in the evenings.

Notes / Birthdays

This terrace is embedded in attractive greenery all year round, thanks to ivy cubes *(Hedera helix* 'Arborescens') and box spheres. Box cones in containers and yew cuboids against the facade complement the interplay of shapes.

Garden: Janny Schrijver (NL)

February

27 February

Many types and varieties of the delicate early spring crocus (such as *Crocus ancyrensis, Crocus angustifolius, Crocus chrysanthus, Crocus flavus)* have yellow blossoms. If you suddenly find the long-awaited sunny blooms lying on the ground in pieces, this is the work of the male blackbird. The Society for Nature Conservation explains this behaviour as a turf war, which can be particularly fierce at the boundaries between territories, as the yellow crocuses resemble the yellow beaks of rival male blackbirds. It's usually possible to discourage the birds by hanging up strips of tinfoil and putting up pinwheels. If this doesn't work, try planting white, light blue and purple varieties next year.

How lucky to be able to look the first crocuses (here: *Crocus chrysanthus* 'Ard Schenk') in the eye! Their grass-like, white-lined leaves, seen here clearly, shouldn't be mowed down – even when the plants are allowed to run wild in lawns – if these early bloomers are to reappear and spread in the following year.

February

28 February

All 22 varieties of cyclamen have disc-shaped or round bulbs and originate from regions of Asia Minor and around the Mediterranean. It comes as no surprise, then, that many of them aren't hardy, above all the Persian cyclamen *(Cyclamen persicum)*. It is, however, possible to grow some varieties in the garden:

- Eastern cyclamen *(Cyclamen coum)* with round, heart-shaped leaves, which blossoms from February to April. Its bulbs should be planted with the roots facing down at a depth of about 5 cm and protected in winter with brushwood.
- Ivy-leaved cyclamen *(Cyclamen hederifolium)* blooms from September to October and has silver-marked, sharp, heart-shaped leaves. Its bulbs have roots on the top and are planted that way up at a depth of about 10 cm.

Notes / Birthdays

Eastern cyclamens *(Cyclamen coum)* need a sheltered spot under shrubs or in front of a wall, so that their gracefully nodding flowers don't fall victim to frost.

February

29 February

Winter bloomers are fascinating and one of nature's most charming tricks to combat winter drabness. But how do their flowers react to frost?

- The white, half-filled blossoms of the winter cherry *(Prunus subhirtella* 'Autumnalis'*)* can flower as early as November. Although they succumb to frost immediately, the buds don't freeze, so new blossoms open regularly.
- Bodnant viburnum *(Viburnum × bodnantense),* Farrer viburnum *(Viburnum farreri)* and wintersweet *(Chimonanthus praecox)* need a sheltered location or should be planted in mild winter climates, since their flowers tolerate only a light frost.
- Lower sub-zero temperatures, on the other hand, can be tolerated by the blossoms of witch hazel *(Hamamelis),* snowdrops and Christmas roses *(Helleborus).*

The robust buttercup witch hazel *(Corylopsis pauciflora)* is only 1.5 metres tall and blooms from March onwards. But its yellow bunches of flowers can only really be enjoyed in regions with mild winter climates, as sub-zero temperatures quickly damage them. They should be covered with fleece on frosty nights.

February

1 March

Snowdrop days and snowdrop markets attract more and more visitors every year. However, beginners often find it hard to induce these graceful harbingers of spring to grow in the garden. This is usually because they're planted too late and the small bulbs have become too dry. They should be planted as early as possible (in other words, in late August/early September). The second safe method is to buy small pregrown flowering plants in pots now and then plant them once the soil is no longer frozen. The quickest way to form a carpet of snowdrops is to cut off fist-size pieces from old clusters in May/June and plant them immediately.

Notes / Birthdays

Snowdrop *(Galanthus)* seeds contain delicacies for ants. They carry them off and detach the treasured appendage, causing the seeds to start germinating in random places.

Garden and design: Peter Janke (D)

March

2 March

Shrubs begin to sprout with surprising force as soon as the frost leaves the ground. The power to do this varies depending on the species and variety. Some shrubs can even penetrate tarred surfaces and eliminate weaker neighbours. That's why it's important to look closely to find out which shrubs are getting too large and should be reduced in size or rejuvenated. It's also worthwhile to become acquainted with the shoots and young foliage of the plants to make sure they're not mistaken for weeds during weeding.

Notes / Birthdays

The shoots of this euphorbia *(Euphorbia griffithii* 'Dixter') push up through the ground like rockets. The reddish colour (from anthocyanins) is one of its survival strategies and protects the plant from UV light and sunburn.

March

3 March

When the crocuses are in bloom, it's time to cut back ornamental grasses. Even dead stalks prevent moisture and cold from penetrating into the rootstock during the winter. Now you should cut the grasses back to about 15 cm above the ground using garden shears, a scythe or electric hedge clippers. This must be done early to prevent damage to the young shoots. Important note: in contrast to ornamental grasses, don't cut back wintergreen and evergreen grasses. Simply comb through the clusters with your hand and remove the dead matter.

Notes / Birthdays

These two clusters of Chinese Silver Grass *(Miscanthus)* have fulfilled their task of enlivening the garden with two impressive vertical sculptures.
Garden and design: Peter Janke (D)

March

4 March

Year in, year out, witch hazel *(Hamamelis × intermedia)* with its early blooms wakes the garden from its winter sleep. Depending on the variety, this robust and completely winter-hardy shrub blooms in yellow, orange or red from February to April. It takes a long time to grow to its picturesque overhanging shape, so it should be left as a solitary shrub and not be cut back. In autumn, it bids farewell with the fiery golden spectacle of its rough, hazel-nut-like leaves.

Notes / Birthdays

Red and orange blooming varieties of witch hazel ('Diane' in this case) are a good choice for close to the house because their filigree blooms contrast fragrantly with light-coloured walls and facades.

March

5 March

The resting period for green thumbs is over. You can now spruce up potted plants in their winter quarters, put them in a lighter place and water them more. Repotting is due every three to four years. If you want to keep a pot which is already quite large, just reduce the size of the root ball. To do this, remove a thick slice at the base with a knife and cut off pieces at the sides too. A root ball cut back in this way fits into the same pot with the addition of fresh substrate. All that's left to do now is to water it well and keep the plant in a shady and protected place for at least two weeks.

Notes / Birthdays

On this evergreen terrace with its ivy *(Hedera)* and its boxwood stems, snowdrops and filled hellebores *(Helleborus)* are attracting the first bees. Potted tulips and daffodils will soon bring brilliant colours to the terrace.
Garden and design: Peter Janke (D)

March

6 March

To ensure that strawberries are healthy and fertile at the start of the season, you should now cut back old leaves and push plants lifted by frost back into the soil. Then hoe the soil between the rows of strawberries, remove the weeds, and work in compost or a special strawberry fertiliser around the plants.

Notes / Birthdays

The large-bloomed crocus 'Jeanne d'Arc' really begins to shine when the evening comes. It looks great from a distance too – even for pollinators, for whom pistils and stamens with their garish neon orange colour promise a mouth-watering meal.

March

7 March

From mid-March onwards, you can pregrow summer flowers and vegetables on the window ledge. Use special low-nutrient sowing earth for sowing. In spite of this, the seedlings often grow to be long, thin and crooked. This is the fault of the still "weak" light falling on the window ledge from one side only. However, if you put the seed trays into a box open at the front and covered with aluminium foil at the back, you'll be more successful. The aluminium foil reflects the incident light so that the seedlings are exposed to light from behind too. This encourages them to grow straight and strong.

Notes / Birthdays

In the sheltered microclimate of a light-flooded greenhouse, it's not only sowing time. Young plants purchased pregrown also find an optimum nursery here.
Garden: Regina Vylsteke (B)

March

8 March

Small walls, tables and stands are the perfect places for an impressive display of spring flowers, for they bring the dainty blooms close to the eye and the nose. You can put them into containers of matching shades of colour or use ones with strong contrasts instead – it's entirely up to you.

However, a small trick improves their appearance: the more colourful the plants in the pot garden are, the more uniform the colour and material of the containers should be. In this way, you can design enchanting flower arrangements for all seasons.

Notes / Birthdays

When the garden is still bare, you can add colour by using various containers. Here, a blue band of grape hyacinths *(Muscari)* adorns the wall. After flowering, the plants are put into flower beds or bedded out and allowed to run to seed.
Garden: De Keukenhof (NL)

March

9 March

You can plant trees and shrubs as soon as the ground has thawed. Maybe this is just the right moment to give a pond a vertical counterpoint in the form of a striking solitary tree. Trees with several trunks or overhanging trees look especially picturesque close to the pond. However, ornamental grasses, bamboo, large shrubs or shrub roses can do the job too. It's important to consider the proportions here. A large pond, for example, can take a high and spreading tree or shrub close to it. By contrast, a small pond should only be accompanied by a moderately high tree such as a Japanese maple *(Acer palmatum* 'Dissectum') or a hanging goat willow *(Salix caprea* 'Pendula').

Notes / Birthdays

The mighty white willow *(Salix alba* 'Tristis') is a romantic eye-catcher in this landscaped garden with its large pond.
Garden: Emy and Peter Ultee (NL), design: In Goede Aarde (NL)

March

10 March

Not only beekeepers know how hard it is for bees and other pollinating insects to find food, especially after the winter rest. So why not plant early flowering shrubs which give the gardener a lot of pleasure and provide the bees with nourishment in early spring? These all-rounders include flowering quince *(Chaenomeles)*, Cornelian cherry *(Cornus mas)*, buttercup witch hazel *(Corylopsis pauciflora)*, alpine heather *(Erica carnea)*, Bodnant viburnum *(Viburnum × bodnantense)* and Farrer's viburnum *(Viburnum farreri)*.

Notes / Birthdays

An early delicacy par excellence for bees: the Japanese dragon willow *(Salix udensis/sachalinensis* 'Sekka') with its especially large catkins on the still bare and often bizarrely flattened and twisted shoots.

March

11 March

After thorough preparation, a colourful sea of flowers can now shine splendidly on the grass or under deciduous trees and shrubs. Almost all harbingers of spring with enough strength to break through the turf are suitable for bedding out and running to seed. By contrast, highly bred varieties of tulips, daffodils and crown imperials require comfortable conditions in the flower beds.

For freestyle planting in the grass, remove the sods in September and loosen the uncovered earth. Then scatter the bulbs, leaving them to lie where they fall, and cover them up with the sods. As soon as the shoot apexes peep out of the soil in spring, spread organic fertiliser over a wide area.

Notes / Birthdays

Here, bulbs of the large-flower varieties 'Flower Record' (striped) and 'Pickwick' (purple) were mixed before being scattered. To make sure they bloom every year, however, you must wait until after the white-lined crocus petals are retracted before mowing.
Garden: De Keukenhof (NL)

March

12 March

After severe winters, algae can bloom in ponds in early spring. The reason for this is the lack of oxygen in winter. As the underwater plants cannot produce any oxygen under a blanket of ice, many small creatures die there and form organic slime rich in nutrients. After the thaw, the light returns to the pond, allowing the algae present in this paradise of light and nutrients to turn into dense carpets in a short time. Clean off the algae. The animal and plant worlds usually regulate themselves after a certain time. However, if the plague of algae continues, you should measure the water values and resort to corrective measures if necessary.

Notes / Birthdays

Water features should always go with the style of the garden, like this rectangular pool, which blends in perfectly with the modern formal structure of the garden.

Garden: Landesgartenschau Zülpich, design: GartenLandschaft Berg (D)

March

13 March

When the open-air season begins, some people fancy having weatherproof outdoor wicker furniture made of polyrattan. This is not a uniform material but deceptively similar rattan imitations made of various artificial fibres based on polyethylene. The "chemical recipe", the name of the fibres, their width, the braiding style and the design of the furniture differ depending on the manufacturer. Its popularity is understandable. In contrast to natural fibres, it's rainproof and tear-resistant, UV- and temperature-resistant, lightweight and easy to clean. If little room is available, however, you should use space-saving stackable or folding furniture or seat combinations (usually made of a mixture of materials).

Notes / Birthdays

As an outside living room, an open pavilion provides shelter from sun and rain without obstructing the view. At the same time, it provides an appropriate setting for bulky lounge furniture.
Garden: Sarina Meijer (NL), design: A. J. van der Horst (NL)

March

14 March

If you choose the plants cleverly, you can create especially striking combinations in flower beds or pots. It's important to have detailed botanical knowledge of colours, growth heights and florescences – the same applies to bulb flowers and their many varieties. Partners with the same florescence can produce subtle colour effects in combined flower beds. By contrast, partners with a staggered florescence extend the blossom period of a flower bed and – depending on the flowers selected – even allow for a change of colour.

Notes / Birthdays

When the two-coloured Candia tulip *(Tulipa saxatilis,* formerly *bakeri)* 'Lilac Wonder' ends its appearance in April, the fragrant angel's tears daffodil 'Hawera' opens its folded-back light yellow blooms until early May.

March

15 March

Small early spring flowers are most effective in large numbers. You don't necessarily need to plant them as carpets of flowers, but they should at least be in small clusters. Then they spread further from year to year at a site that takes their fancy. Be they winter aconites *(Eranthis hyemalis)*, wood anemones *(Anemone nemorosa)*, sweet violets *(Viola odorata)*, spring snowflakes *(Leucojum vernum)* or common snowdrops *(Galanthus nivalis)*, they're all team players and are perfect for the space below the still bare and transparent deciduous trees and shrubs – as solitaires, groups or hedges. The magic is over in June, when all but the winter-green sweet violet have lost their foliage.

Notes / Birthdays

With its brilliant blue colour, the winter windflower *(Anemone blanda)* announces the joy of spring in bowls and baskets too. After the blossom, you can plant it at the edge of deciduous trees and let it run to seed.

March

16 March

As soon as the soil has thawed and dried off, you can prepare vegetable patches for planting. To encourage their natural fertility, loosen the soil while taking care not to overly mix up the soil layers. Heavy soils have to be broken up using a spade. Medium–heavy soils are handled using a digging fork, with which you pierce the soil deeply at intervals of 15–20 cm. The fork is then moved back and forth. A sow tooth is sufficient for working deeply humous soils or light sandy soils. Drag it through the patch in diagonal lines and then once more in the opposite direction to form a lozenge pattern. No matter how you loosen the soil, remove the weeds and mix in compost or an organic compound fertiliser.

Notes / Birthdays

Garden centres and garden markets are now once again places of pure seduction. Why not treat yourself to a visit? These inspiring eldorados encourage you to enjoy gardening.
Garden and design: Peter Janke (D)

March

17 March

Who doesn't want to experience the revival of nature from close quarters? Pregrown plants are just waiting for their chance to represent spring in bowls and pots on balconies and terraces. Pansies, horned pansies and daisies prove to be especially robust against frost and snow. They can be combined with bulb flowers to make enchanting arrangements. Natural materials and accessories in the country-house style underline their spring charm. They seem even more natural if you embed them in moss or ivy, cover them with small grasses and twigs and choose containers made of wicker mesh or bark.

Charming horned pansies *(Viola cornuta)* in blue and violet tones and white grape hyacinths *(Muscari botryoides* 'Album') make a cheerful combination that lasts until early May.

March

18 March

On dry, frost-free days, you can spring-clean the shrub beds. Cut off dead plant parts and loosen the soil around the shrubs. You can remove the weeds easily before spreading compost or fertiliser and working it into the soil. This is also the best time to rejuvenate shrubs by levering over-age clusters out of the soil using a digging fork, dividing them up and replanting parts of them. Wherever there are gaps in the flower bed, there's room for a new garden treasure.

Notes / Birthdays

After the daffodils have flowered, you should cut off the seed pods but never the leaves. If you want to tidy up the bed slightly before the leaves turn brown and are retracted, weave them into small pigtails.

March

19 March

When the days get warmer again, it's time to prepare garden furniture and the terrace for the summer. Clean wood, metal and plastic furniture with soapy water and rinse it off again thoroughly. If you wish to freshen up the warm tone of wooden furniture, leave the paint to dry for a day or two afterwards, then apply wood oil from a specialist shop. If the furniture has already gone grey, this patina must be sanded off before you apply the oil. The same is true for terrace coverings made of wood. Even coverings made of WPC (wood-plastic composite, see 8 May) can turn grey from wind and weather. For these coverings, there are special WPC refreshers which conserve the fresh wood colour of the composite material.

(wood-plastic composite, see 8 May)

Notes / Birthdays

The white of the Triumph Tulip 'White Dream' mixed with the fresh green of boxwood and grass – this formal garden has all it takes to make any gardner's heart miss a beat.
Garden: Christien Reinders (NL)

March

20 March

A dense lawn is a velvety green backdrop for displaying plants and garden elements at their best. Here's the basic procedure to ensure that it continues to thrive impeccably: as soon as the lawn has dried off, rake up any old leaves and twigs. The mowing season starts when the forsythias are in bloom. After mowing, evenly spread long-term lawn fertiliser. Depending on the requirements, also carry out renovation work such as cutting out weeds and repairing damaged patches. Fill up dents in the lawn surface with earth and flatten small mounds raised by frost. Then sow grass seeds in these places, press them down gently with your foot and water the area carefully.

Lawn care also includes cleaning up the edges, for clear contours give structure to lawns and flower beds. These beds are full of yellow Darwin hybrid tulips with their red stripes ('Juliette') and daffodils.
Garden: Addy and Jan Traas (NL)

March

21 March

There's work to be done on the pond from March onwards. As soon as the ice has melted, you should check the bank reinforcement and the edge of the pond. A greatly reduced water level may be a sign that frost has caused the pond liner or capillary barrier to become leaky. The site of the damage is usually indicated by an unusually damp spot along the pond's edge. There's still time to remove old leaves and other organic matter from the pond overflow and sump before the main season begins. Decorative ponds should be cleaned thoroughly before you fill them again. For safety reasons, you should wait until April before reinstalling any technical systems.

Notes / Birthdays

_____

_____

_____

_____

Bulb flowers can be used both as colour and form elements to enrich the garden. Here, they form a yellow-and-white band meandering playfully through a modern and strictly formal arrangement.
Garden: De Heerenhof (NL)

March

22 March

Annual flowers overflow with colour until autumn arrives. If they're to start flowering in May, it's best to begin sowing them out in the house now – or buy pregrown young plants from the garden centre.

Pregrowing plants on the window ledge is recommended for all summer flowers which are later to be included in a shrub bed, since this allows them to better assert themselves against their neighbours. Pregrowing gives annuals such as the floss flower *(Ageratum)*, which requires a longer period of preparation, or annual climbing plants which have to complete a large-scale growth programme a head start with regard to development and blossom.

Notes / Birthdays

A sea of flowers like this one only comes about by direct sowing. First the turf is removed and the soil below loosened. Bachelor's buttons *(Centaurea cyanus)* and common poppies *(Papaver rhoeas)* then flower from June to September and seed themselves in future.
Garden: Nina Balthau (B)

March

23 March

Is it time to cut back the hydrangeas? If so, it's important to know the plants well beforehand. Paniculate hydrangeas *(Hydrangea paniculata)* and common hydrangeas *(Hydrangea arborescens,* such as the 'Annabelle' variety) flower on the new shoots. That's why you should prune the shoots by a good two thirds. Hydrangeas of the Endless Summer and Forever & Ever groups blossom on old and new shoots and can be cut back as far as you like. All other hydrangeas form their flower buds on the previous year's shoots. Here, you need only remove the dried flower heads to reveal a new pair of buds beneath. These include French hydrangeas *(Hydrangea macrophylla)*, mountain hydrangeas *(H. serrata)*, oak-leaved hydrangeas *(H. quercifolia)* and climbing hydrangeas *(H. anomala* subsp. *petiolaris)*.

Notes / Birthdays

The Japanese quince *(Chaenomeles japonica)* blossoms in March on the previous year's shoots – and flowers most richly when it isn't cut back.

24 March

Lawns which are often in the shade or suffer from a lack of nutrients or compacted earth soon become matted and prone to moss. Aerating is necessary here. During this treatment, the knives cut through the matted lawn and score the ground, allowing air, light and nutrients to reach the roots again unimpeded. Don't start aerating until at least two weeks after spreading fertiliser, so that the grass can become stronger after the winter. The lawn should be mowed and dry. Move the aerating device speedily lengthwise across the lawn, and then once more in a crosswise direction. Finally, rake off the matted grass thoroughly.

Notes / Birthdays

A country-house garden with variously shaped shrub beds and a well-kept lawn is an oasis for the senses. If the lawns are large, petrol-driven or electric aerators with a bag to catch the cuttings can save a lot of work.

Garden: Tuin 't Hofje (NL)

March

25 March

As soon as the yellow of the forsythias begins to shine, you can start pruning the roses. This encourages lots of blossoms to form but can also control their growth. Cutting them back strongly, for example, produces fewer, longer and stronger shoots with large blossoms, whereas cutting them back weakly leads to the formation of many thin shoots with a large number of smaller blossoms. This is why weak shoots should be cut back strongly and stronger ones less deeply.

Pruning is always done half a centimetre above one of the leaf buds (which are located on the stems or in the axils) and pointing away from it in a diagonal downward motion. This allows the moisture to run off instead of directing it towards the shoot.

Notes / Birthdays

The fragrant light yellow bells of the early Stachyurus *(Stachyurus praecox)* seem to be lined up on suspended strings of pearls *(Stachyurus praecox)*. This shrub is sensitive to frost, flowers from March to April and delights with a brilliant orangey red in autumn.

March

26 March

It's been a long time since magnolias only flowered in white and pink. If you live in a region with mild winters and wish to have a splendid solitary tree, there are countless varieties to entice you.

- There are dark purplish-red varieties which flower not only during the blossom period between March and May, but once more from June to August too. These include *Magnolia* 'Genie' (extremely winter-hardy), 'Susan' and 'Nigra' (both derivatives of *Magnolia liliiflora)*.
- There are also fragrant yellow hybrids such as 'Daphne' (winter-hardy down to -25°C), 'Sunsation' (yellow with raspberry-coloured stripes), 'Elizabeth' and 'Yellow River' (both light yellow).
- An especially colourful sight is *Magnolia acuminata* 'Blue Opal', whose blue-green buds open to become yellowish-green blossoms.

March

Notes / Birthdays

The buds of the noble tulip magnolia *(Magnolia × soulangeana)* are protected by little fur coats. Unfortunately, the large white or pink blossoms on the ends of the shoots can fall victim to late frosts.

27 March

Summer-flowering shrubs and subshrubs which blossom on new shoots from this year should be cut back strongly now at the latest. Prune back butterfly bush *(Buddleja davidii* hybrids), tree lavatera *(Lavatera thuringiaca)*, hibiscus *(Hibiscus syriacus)*, Californian lilac *(Ceanothus)*, blue spiraea *(Caryopteris)*, lavender *(Lavandula)* and perovskia *(Perovskia)* to a height of about 30 cm, whereas older plants are cut back to just above the woody frame. Low shrubs such as shrubby cinquefoil *(Potentilla fruticosa)*, Japanese spyraea *(Spiraea japonica)* and heather *(Calluna vulgaris)* can even be pruned to 10–15 cm in height using hedge clippers.

Notes / Birthdays

The magnificent foliage of the Japanese maple *(Acer palmatum* 'Dissectum Atropurpureum') is green in summer and surprises with a fiery red in autumn.
Garden: Japanese Garden, Bayer Leverkusen (D)

March

28 March

Unless they're protected by fleece or film, neither potted spring decorations nor young vegetables in vegetable patches are safe from the cold. With potted plants, it's sufficient to cover the plants up carefully with bubble wrap. Permanent fleeces and slit films, which allow light, air and water to get through to the plant, are recommended for vegetable beds. Dig them in on one of the long sides of the patch. On the opposite side, it's enough to weigh them down with stones. This allows you to just throw back the fleece or slit film on nice days.

Notes / Birthdays

What's sprouting here is a monster straight out of hell. It's Chinese rhubarb *(Rheum palmatum* var. *tanguticum),* an impressive shrub with ornamental leaves which grows as high as two metres.

March

29 March

Along the lines of "From nature, for the garden", gardeners in England have always used the long, richly branched shoots one gets after pruning bushes as supporting material for shrubs or peas. In flower beds, press the cuttings into the soil around any shrub which is not quite self-supporting, snap off the shoots in the upper third and interweave them horizontally. The result is a stable supporting cage through which the plant can grow.

In the case of peas, the shoots are put into the ground in rows about 50 cm apart. Only then do you start sowing. Important note: the supports require a certain stability so that the tendrils of the growing peas find a firm foothold in wind and rain. Copper beech shoots, for example, are suitable here.

Notes / Birthdays

You can hardly tell that the pompoms of the filled daisies *(Bellis perennis)* are related to the plain daisy. One trait they do have in common, though, is their robustness against snow and cold.

March

30 March

The increasing popularity of hellebores (*Helleborus* orientalis hybrids) is reflected in the widening range of varieties. Aside from white and greenish flowers, there are also simple and filled ones in red, violet, yellow and orange tones – and they can also have different-coloured stripes, dots or borders. Hellebore lovers often regret being unable to look into the nodding faces of these little beauties without being reminded that they're one of nature's precautionary measures – enabling the outer petals to protect the fructificative organs so that they can be pollinated even after rain or frost. To ensure that they still look good, just remove the foliage which becomes unsightly in winter.

'Anemone-flowering' is the name for the form of the bloom of this otherwise nameless hellebore, in which dark, enlarged nectaries surround stamens and carpels like a ruff.

March

31 March

Now is the time to plant roses. Don't let your enthusiasm for a new variety be dampened by lack of space! There are still plenty of possibilities in a vertical direction. Climbing roses and ramblers don't need much space and can romantically cover entire facades, walls and garden sheds, provided that the walls are oriented towards the south-west or south-east. Walls facing south must be in the shade in the midday heat, otherwise the dry air and heat accumulation can easily make the roses fall ill. It's important to have a trellis which gives the shoots a stable foothold and is sufficiently far away from the wall to allow air to circulate behind the plant too.

Notes / Birthdays

The rambler rose 'New Dawn' is suitable even for facades with a lot of windows. Vertically guided shoots easily become bare. However, horizontally guided shoots above the windows cause an accumulation of sap, which yields a large number of flowering side shoots.
Garden: Visser family (NL)

March

1 April

If you only do your gardening at ground level, you're missing out on some wonderful creative opportunities. This is because a garden doesn't become a welcoming place until it is divided up by vertical elements and high plants and turned into a self-contained space. The trick is to integrate space-saving height elements like solitary trees, obelisks, trimmed hedges, trellises and rose arches into small refuges. Large gardens can also be subdivided into room-like spaces by freely growing hedges or groups of trees, and the pathways can be covered with a pergola, a pavilion or a series of rose arches.

Notes / Birthdays

Even when the beech hedges and roses on the pavilion and arches have not yet sprouted, they still subdivide the formal country-house garden into self-contained spaces.
Garden: Christien Reinders (NL)

April

2 April

Even before the forsythias, the Cornelian cherry *(Cornus mas)* covers itself with pale yellow veils of flowers, followed by edible fruits from August onwards and an orangey-yellow autumn colouring starting in October. The elongated red stone fruits contain a lot of vitamin C and can be used to make juice, jam or chutney – but they can also be enjoyed in the fresh or dried state. 'Jolico' and 'Golden Glory' are large-fruit varieties. The plant takes well to cutting back and has much to offer from a creative point of view too, whether as a solitaire, in a wild or trimmed hedge or even on a trellis or pergola.

Notes / Birthdays

The flower umbels of the Cornelian cherry are a magnet for bees and bumble-bees. Later in the year, birds and small mammals appreciate its acidic fruits.

3 April

If it rains frequently at cherry blossom time, you should keep a watchful eye on fruit trees and ornamental varieties alike. This is because rain during the blossom period allows spores of the fungus *Monilia laxa* to enter especially easily. The first signs of this are dying shoot apexes which rapidly turn brown towards the inside. Cut the twigs affected by dryness of the apex back 20 cm into the healthy wood and burn the cuttings. If the tree is severely afflicted, cut back all flowering twigs. Before the year is out, the tree will form new shoots which will blossom the following year.

Notes / Birthdays

The Japanese cherry 'Kanzan' *(Prunus serrulata)* – also known as carnation cherry due to the form and fragrance of its double blooms – is wide and funnel-shaped and grows to a height of 10 metres.

April

4 April

As early as April – even before the mountain clematis *(Clematis montana)*, that is – the graceful varieties of alpine clematis *(Clematis alpina)* blossom on shoots with a length of 2–3.5 metres. This clematis group doesn't need to be cut back, is robust and winter-hardy and even tolerates permanent shade and dry places, for example in front of woody plants or under overhanging roofs. Its suspended blooms with long points often even appear once again in August. These *Ranunculaceae* can be presented most attractively on trellises which aren't too thick and look decorative in winter too.

Notes / Birthdays

From late April onwards, mountain clematis *(Clematis montana)* weaves a pale pink border around nesting boxes and plant arrangements on house walls.
Garden: Elisabeth Imig and Silke Imig-Gerold (D)

April

5 April

Clematis doesn't need much ground space, but it requires a trellis. This is put into place before you plant the clematis. To prevent the shoots from bending, use the supporting stick to fix the trellis in the ground in as vertical a position as possible. The soil should be rich in humus and loosened down to a depth of 80 cm, so that one to two pairs of eyes additionally go into the earth at the base. The wet-sensitive alpine and mountain clematis must also be provided with drainage when used in heavy compacted soils. If the clematis is to climb on deciduous trees, plant it in a 10-litre bucket without a bottom so that it can grow without troublesome root pressure.

Notes / Birthdays

A place to sit under mountain clematis *(Clematis montana)* intoxicates the senses if you choose a fragrant variety such as 'Pink Perfection', 'Tetra Rose', 'Odorata' (all pink) or 'Alexander' (white).
Garden: Schlosspark Benrath (D)

April

6 April

Now the garden pond is awaking to new life. At the water's edge, cut the dead stalks of reeds, grasses and rushes back to the base to give the young shoots light and space.

You can reinstall the technical equipment in the pond from April onwards. Check pumps and filters before installing. Fountains and water features can now come back to burbling life again at last. Pond filters should be cleaned after the first four weeks.

Notes / Birthdays

The spatial design of this modern garden is not just made up of lawn, sandy patch, cut hedge and concrete wall, but also includes water in various geometrical settings.

Garden: Chelsea Flower Show, design: Luciano Giubbilei (GB), sculpture: Ursula von Rydingsvard (USA)

April

7 April

After the tulips and daffodils flower, cut off the withered parts and seed pods so that they don't sap the strength of the plants unnecessarily. At the same time, you should apply a full mineral fertiliser, the nutrients of which are stored by the bulb plants with the help of their leaves. That's why the latter should never be cut off before they are retracted. To prevent the leaves from making herbaceous borders look untidy in this period, tulips and daffodils should be planted in the centre or at the back so that the sprouting shrubs cover up the yellowing leaves.

Notes / Birthdays

A potpourri of purple tulips and forget-me-nots *(Myosotis sylvatica)* is a cheerful sight in this cottage garden. Before and behind them, the shoots of the summer shrubs are advancing.
Garden: Thea and Dirk Maldegem (NL)

April

8 April

When designing a herbaceous border, you should consider the effects of colour too. Whereas strong contrasts (such as complementary colours) seem dynamic and full of tension, harmonious colour compositions are soothing to eye and soul. Such fine plays of colour mostly come into being thanks to tone-in-tone flower beds or combinations which produce a colour gradient. Tone-in-tone arrangements play with different brightness levels of one single colour, whereas colour gradients usually operate with three neighbouring colours in the chromatic circle, such as red, orange and yellow.

This purple tone-in-tone ensemble is indeed a refreshing sight! The Triumph tulips 'Dreaming Maid' (light purple) and 'Negrita' (dark purple) are joined by the petite blossoms of honesty *(Lunaria annua)*.

April

9 April

Sweet violets *(Viola odorata)* are considered the epitome of modesty. If they find good growing conditions, however, they'll spread cheerfully throughout the garden – aided and abetted by ants who carry their seeds away. It does no harm to harvest a few of their leaves to make salads or candy their blossoms for desserts and cakes. To do this, spread them with egg white, sprinkle refined sugar on them and let them dry through.

The healing powers of violets were described in the writings of visionary Hildegard von Bingen. Today we know that they form circular protein molecules (so-called cyclotides) which it may soon be possible to use against cancer, autoimmune diseases and virus infections.

Notes / Birthdays

With their fantastic colours and patterns, auriculas *(Primula auricula)* form a world of their own that collectors pamper in pots. The 'White Wings' variety looks as if it's covered in flour.

April

10 April

If you want to plant a flowering cherry, you should consider not just the colour of the flower (white and light or vivid pink) and the size of the tree, but also the shape it grows to. The Japanese cherry *Prunus serrulata* 'Amanogawa' is slim enough to fit into small front gardens.

Weeping varieties look picturesque at the water's edge. Examples are *Prunus subhirtella* 'Pendula', *Prunus serrulata* 'Kiku–Shidare-Zakura' and *Prunus × yedoensis* 'Ivensii'.

Funnel-shaped flowering cherries with a wide crown or several trunks are predestined to be solitaires and eye-catchers. They include varieties of *Prunus serrulata* such as 'Kanzan', 'Pink Perfection', 'Shirofugen', 'Taihaku' and *Prunus subhirtella* 'Fukubana'.

Notes / Birthdays

A Cheal's weeping cherry *(Prunus serrulata* 'Kiku- Shidare-Zakura')* gracefully bends its filled pink blossoms over a stream.
Garden: Japanese Garden Bayer Leverkusen (D)

April

11 April

When choosing new shrubs, grasses or ferns, you should not only find out about suitable locations, colours, florescence and height, but also ascertain whether their growth is described as "clump-like" or as "forming runners". This is because shrubs which form runners soon "overrun" their neighbours. The smaller a garden is, the more time you'll need to keep these plants in check. For small gardens and low-maintenance vegetation, therefore, it's recommended to choose plants with "clump-like" growth.

Notes / Birthdays

When it unfurls its new fronds, the ostrich fern *(Matteuccia struthiopteris)* forms beautiful, evenly growing funnels. Unfortunately, its creeping rhizomes allow it to spread very easily.

April

12 April

You can make dahlias blossom earlier by propagating the tubers. First remove mouldy or withered parts and then put the bulbs into water for a few hours so that they can fill with liquid. Then, for each plant, put fresh potting compost into a pot until it's three-quarters full and plant the tubers with the eyes facing upwards. Cover everything up with compost, which you push down slightly and water gently. Then set up the pots in a light place at room temperature. The sprouting dahlia shouldn't be planted out until late April to mid-May.

Notes / Birthdays

The cheerful character of spring is embodied by this garden with its colourful confetti-like ensemble of tulips, daffodils and honesty *(Lunaria annua)*.
Garden: Elisabeth Imig and Silke Imig-Gerold (D)

April

13 April

Choose a dry, overcast day for pruning the roses. Use the shears for garden roses and floribunda and for frequently flowering shrub roses and climbing roses. Remove dead and over-age shoots from all your roses. Leave garden roses and floribunda three eyes per shoot and cut back shrub roses by a third. Spare the long shoots of climbing roses which flower frequently. However, you can cut the side shoots back to two to four sprouting buds.

Notes / Birthdays

_____

_____

_____

_____

A wide-crowned flowering cherry is a picturesque tree for close to the house. It shines over the terrace with fragrant clouds of blossoms in spring and colourful foliage in autumn.
Garden: Nina Balthau (B)

April

14 April

No matter whether they consist of herbs, flowers or plant collections in pots – pot gardens should always be a decorative eye-catcher. They gain in charm if you arrange your green treasures at different heights using stands, racks, columns or higher plant pots. It's also important for your little mobile garden to have a connecting motif. This can be achieved using two or more recurring colours, but also by choosing pots made of similar materials or colours.

Notes / Birthdays

A coating of moss on the work table, wreaths and baskets made of wickerwork as well as pots with earth-coloured rust-brown patina underline the enchanting naturalness of this still life with spring flowers.
Garden: Elisabeth Imig and Silke Imig-Gerold (D)

April

15 April

To ensure that climbing and rambler roses flower profusely on arches, pergolas or pavilions, it's now time to guide them upwards correctly. After thinning them out and pruning them, tie the long shoots upwards. Don't guide them up vertically, however, but wind them around the trellis like a spiral between small brackets to keep them growing as horizontally as possible. This causes congestion of the sap, which brings forth new side shoots so that the lower part of the rose can flower too.

Notes / Birthdays

Long before the roses on the pavilion open their flowers, this rural idyll has turned into a fragrant little garden. From April to June, purple and white dame's violet *(Hesperis matronalis* and 'Alba' variety) give off their enchanting fragrance in the evening hours.
Garden: Elisabeth Imig and Silke Imig-Gerold (D)

April

16 April

As standard plants, berry bushes can be made suitable for flower gardens in a variety of ways. In the form of miniature trees, you can use redcurrants or gooseberries to accentuate the centre point of a circular flower bed, mark the beginning of a pathway as a duo or arch over entire beds to form a small avenue. Being self-seeding, even solitary plants in large pots can bear fruit. However, they bear more fruit when mixed with other varieties. A supporting stick is sufficient for young stems. To prevent large crowns bearing a lot of fruit from bending, you should build a three-legged support around the foot so that the upper slats can support the crown.

Notes / Birthdays

Pear trees climbing artfully up a pergola provide blossoms, shade and fruit depending on the season. In spring, daffodils and forget-me-nots surround its bare base.
Garden: Thea and Dirk Maldegem (NL)

April

17 April

Mint *(Mentha)* enriches flower beds and kitchens with the incredible variety of its foliage and a huge range of minty aromas. Now it's planting time for these leafy beauties. They love moist soils rich in humus in semi-shady places and can become up to 80 cm high depending on the variety. As many of them proliferate quickly, you have to curb their spread in the flower bed. It's best to plant them out in large mortar buckets with holes in the bottom or cultivate in large pots from the start, where they can even spend the winter outdoors.

Notes / Birthdays

Like all magnolias, the northern Japanese magnolia *(Magnolia kobus)* with its delicate fragrance has shallow roots, so nothing should be planted underneath it.

April

18 April

You can prepare robust potted plants for summer now. These include bay *(Laurus nobilis)*, common olive *(Olea europaea)*, oleander *(Nerium oleander)*, camellia *(Camellia)* and pomegranate *(Punica granatum)*. The plants must be protected from direct sunlight for at least two weeks. Otherwise they could easily catch sunburn, which manifests itself as yellow and brown patches on the leaves. Put the plants up against the wall of the house, where they're protected from wind and frost. In nights with sub-zero temperatures, cover them with fleece or film.

Notes / Birthdays

The beauty of its semi-filled blooms in luminous mother-of-pearl pink and its tolerance of frost down to -15°C make the camellia 'Hagoromo' *(Camellia japonica)* a real garden treasure for mild regions.

April

19 April

It's now time to plant hydrangeas *(Hydrangea)* and spread fertiliser around them. These magnificent shrubs love a moist and slightly acidic environment rich in humus (with the exception of the climbing hydrangea, which also tolerates chalky soil). Rhododendron or hydrangea soil is recommended for improving the earth in the garden and planting shrubs in large pots. Hydrangeas already planted out in the garden are now given a head start using slow-release rhododendron fertiliser, whereas liquid hydrangea fertiliser is a better choice for plants in large pots.

Notes / Birthdays

Even if it takes its time at first, the climbing hydrangea *(Hydrangea anomala* subsp. *petiolaris)* soon covers entire walls and sheds. In autumn, its foliage shines forth in brilliant yellow.

Garden: Heiderose Birkenstock (D)

April

20 April

The dandelion *(Taraxacum)* is an undesirable visitor to the garden. Its tap root can grow to a length of more than one metre, allowing it to spread stubbornly through lawns and herbaceous borders. If you want to burn it, you should cut it out deeply before it flowers if possible, otherwise it will seed itself as quick as a flash. Gourmets wishing to use it for salads instead should simply put a bucket or flower-pot over the shoots. The bleached leaves taste more refined and less bitter. However, don't forget to cut off all blooms and buds regularly to avoid seedlings in other parts of the garden.

The long-spurned blooms of barrenwort *(Epimedium franchetii* 'Brimstone Butterfly') are reminiscent of spiders. In April/May, their light yellow colour contrasts distinctively with the large reddish brown leaves. Later, the foliage of this attractive ground cover will turn green.

April

21 April

Bark mulch keeps the soil moist and prevents weeds from growing. You shouldn't use it to cover up shrub beds and vegetable patches, however. This is because bark mulch takes nitrogen from the soil, often contains growth-stunting tannic acid and is frequently contaminated with the heavy metal cadmium. This is released from the ground by acidic forest soil and is absorbed via the tree roots and stored in the bark. If you use it for mulching, cadmium can end up in your home-grown vegetables. Wood chips and dried grass cuttings are more suitable for shrub beds and vegetable patches, whereas straw can also be used for strawberries and raspberries.

Notes / Birthdays

Yellow, white and blue are a guarantee for fragrant spring ensembles. Here, they're provided by daffodils 'Hawera' (yellow), 'Pueblo' (white), blue wood forget-me-nots *(Myosotis sylvatica)*, Burkwood viburnum *(Viburnum × burkwoodii)* and yellow Caucasian leopard's bane *(Doronicum orientale)*.
Garden: Thea and Dirk Maldegem (NL)

22 April

Fine seeds (like those of carrots) are available in convenient forms which make sowing easier. In the case of pilled seed, the seeds are enlarged to a uniform pill format using a soluble pelleting substance which can also include fertilisers and pesticides. This makes them easier to sow evenly.

In seed carpets, the seeds are embedded in cellulose with the optimum spacing for sowing in grooves, so it's no longer necessary to thin them out after germination.

Notes / Birthdays

Once these two children of nature have settled, you don't need to sow any seeds to help them along: forget-me-nots *(Myosotis sylvatica)* and common cowslips *(Primula veris)* are self-seeding plants.

23 April

There's still time to plant or renew a herbaceous border. Plants have an especially attractive effect if you arrange them at different heights. High plants are placed at the back and low ones at the front. Select a maximum of three colours that keep on recurring in different shapes and sizes of flower. If you plant low, small-flowered shrubs in larger quantities and higher, more striking shrubs in smaller ensembles, wonderfully balanced floral arrangements are the result. If you then repeat groups of plants like leitmotifs in large herbaceous borders, you can give the sea of colour rhythm and dynamics.

Notes / Birthdays

In this country-house garden, the arrangement of spring flowers around the fountain includes tulips in purple ('Negrita') and pink ('Mistress'), filled white daffodils ('Bridal Crown'), forget-me-nots (*Myosotis sylvatica*) and dames's violets (*Hesperis matronalis*).
Garden: Elisabeth Imig and Silke Imig-Gerold (D)

24 April

If you want to plant roses, you should be familiar with the phenomenon of soil fatigue. Who hasn't already observed that plants wither or die when planted at a place where another specimen was growing beforehand? This is especially noticeable in the case of roses. Possible causes are incompatible metabolic secretions and a change in the optimum soil condition. That's why you should give each rose a new place to grow if possible. However, if it's absolutely necessary for it to occupy the site of a predecessor – for example on an arch or pergola or in a herbaceous border – the earth must be replaced two spades deep by new soil.

Notes / Birthdays

Above a sea of forget-me-nots (*Myosotis sylvatica*), the tulip 'Synaeda Amor' and the multiflorous tazetta daffodil 'Cragford' spread a delicate scent and provide chromatic elegance.

April

25 April

The pond needs your attention now too. As long as everything isn't covered in green yet, you can thin out plants proliferating in the water and at the water's edge. A rule of thumb says that plants with strong growth should be cut back every three years. To do this, transfer water plants from their pots to baskets, divide them up and put the resulting parts back into place. To divide up freely seeded plants growing at the edge of the pond, detach them carefully from the tangled root felt without damaging the pond liner.

Notes / Birthdays

Even a miniature pond delights the eye and attracts birds and small animals like a small oasis. Thirsty shrubs such as marsh marigold *(Caltha palustris)*, elephant's ear *(Bergenia)* and great cowslip *(Primula elatior)* feel at home at the edge of the pond.
Garden: Elisabeth Imig and Silke Imig-Gerold (D)

April

26 April

Crown imperials *(Fritillaria imperialis)* are the most striking bulb flowers to be seen in spring. The available varieties don't just come in yellow, orange and red – some also have leaves with light stripes as well as striped blossoms ('Striped Beauty'), an old double-crowned variety called 'Kroon op Kroon' (now: 'Prolifera') and the creamy white hybrid 'Early Romance'. They all look magnificent from a distance, so they can be used for the background of the garden. This isn't a bad idea, for their strong garlic-type smell doesn't just repel voles – they would also be troublesome close to the terrace and the sitting area.

Notes / Birthdays

The orange of the crown imperials is taken up by the lily-flowered tulip 'Ballerina' and the small crowns of the tazetta daffodil 'Hoopoe'. The tulip 'Passionale' adds strong purple accents to the colour scheme.

Garden: De Keukenhof (NL),
design: Jacqueline van der Kloet (NL)

April

27 April

When the open-air season begins, some feel the need to screen their garden from view. However, small gardens in particular should never be cordoned off uniformly, as this can make them seem oppressive and closed in. It's much more pleasant to use dividing elements which interrupt continuous surfaces and can be varied. Integrated vistas, diversified green areas with climbing woody plants or shrubs with flowers in front of them are some of the principal ways of breaking up continuous surfaces.

Notes / Birthdays

This is a modern space divider, but it still fits harmoniously into the near-natural environment. It's made possible by the earthy look of the corten steel frames and their filling of logs.
Garden: De Keukenhof (NL)

April

28 April

To help your rhododendrons to flower magnificently, you should now spread fertiliser on these evergreen shrubs. The best way is to spread a slow-release rhododendron fertiliser evenly and work it superficially into the earth. Subsequently, over a period of three months, the fertiliser gradually releases the nutrients to the plants in the exact composition and dosage required by the variety in question. Then lightly water the area spread with fertiliser. Incidentally, larger leaves require more nutrients than smaller ones do.

Notes / Birthdays

This dream team of the semi-shade consisting of hellebores *(Helleborus)*, primroses *(Primula vulgaris* 'Atrosanguinea') and Rodger's bronze-leaf *(Rodgersia podophylla* 'Rotlaub') appears to be covered in a purple veil.
Garden: Geke Rook (NL)

April

29 April

No matter how useful a mulch covering is for fruit trees in summer, you should still do without it for a time in regions susceptible to late frost. This is because the mulch covering stores humidity which freezes at sub-zero temperatures, and the cold is radiated to trees and flowers. It shouldn't be applied until late April to mid-May, when frost is no longer to be expected – but the weeds on the tree bases have to be removed beforehand.

Notes / Birthdays

The graceful snake's head fritillary *(Fritillaria meleagris)* is most effective in large numbers. If its bulbs are planted in moist loamy soil at locations in the semi-shade in August, they become robust and long-lasting.

Garden: Locus Flevum (NL)

April

30 April

Just as the contrast of work and play and of movement and rest makes our lives rich and balanced, the contrast between fullness and emptiness or variety and uniformity is what makes a beautiful garden complete. This is because the one sets the scene for the other. The two complementary units are often lawns and herbaceous borders. In modern gardens, however, groups of grasses or trees can find a tranquil counterpart in paved or gravel-covered areas or water features. If you keep this polarity in mind, harmonious ensembles will virtually come into being by themselves.

Notes / Birthdays

You can see into it from all sides, so the birds are sure to want to move in. In the herbaceous border, it suffices as a solitary accent above the sprouting shrubs.
Garden: Ilka Dorn (D)

April

1 May

The apple blossom marks the beginning of full springtime. Depending on the climate and the region, it can occur at quite different times. Apple trees in the south-west and on the lower Rhine, for example, often open their flowers in late March, whereas they don't blossom in Vaasa, Finland, until the end of May. The apple blossom marks an important time at which gardeners can attend to the following:

• Sowing parsley and nasturtiums
• Cutting back boxwood for the first time
• Checking crown imperials and lily shoots for infestation with red lily beetle
• Replanting a lawn.

Notes / Birthdays

Like a fairy circle, a white-and-yellow band of daffodils frames this seat beneath the fragrant clouds of cherry tree blossom.
Garden: Elisabeth Imig and Silke Imig-Gerold (D)

May

2 May

Owners of small gardens tend to think that they have to do without a fruit tree harvest of their own for lack of space. However, if you're prepared to spend a lot of time maintaining them and cutting them back, you can shape apple and pear trees into trellis hedges, walls or bowers of fruit trees. This requires you to install a stable trellis – one that's attractive in the winter too and matches the style of the garden – before you plant the trees. You should also find a dealer to give you details on varieties recommended for your region and pruning methods which encourage fructification and inhibit their growth.

Notes / Birthdays

In May, these bowers provide fragrant apple blossoms at eye and nose level. In autumn, when the apples ripen, they turn into a veritable land of plenty.
Garden: Nina Balthau (B)

3 May

Compost is often quite rightly known as gardener's gold, for it encourages life in the soil and stimulates the natural fertility of the earth. Mature compost is always sieved before use and should never remain uncovered. To activate and improve the soil, work small quantities into the bed down to a depth of 5–10 cm. Compost can also be used to boost the plants directly if you mix it into the planting soil. It's especially popular in vegetable gardens. Many gardeners line the seed furrows with it when sowing seed or put a shovelful of it into the planting hole to kick-start vegetables with a high or medium-high nutrient consumption.

Notes / Birthdays

Dame's violet *(Hesperis matronalis)*, whose fragrant white and purple flowers bridge the gap between spring and summer blossoms, is a favourite in country-house gardens.
Garden: Elisabeth Imig and Silke Imig-Gerold (D)

May

4 May

Red lettuces speckle vegetable gardens with vivid accents. However, the soil around the supports for runner beans and scarlet runner beans is still bare at the moment. In cold regions in particular, you shouldn't sow them before the end of May. Lay clusters of 5 to 7 beans each around a pole or a rope and they'll wind their way up it in a counter-clockwise direction. In contrast to bush beans, climbing beans also provide original creative possibilities, even outside of vegetable patches. For example, they can climb up obelisks in flower beds, arch over pathways on rose arches or function as space dividers on trellises.

Notes / Birthdays

This fruit and vegetable garden reflects the love of plants typical of the countryside: a beech hedge keeps off cold side winds, while rose arches and herbaceous borders give it a flowery setting.
Garden: Elisabeth Imig and Silke Imig-Gerold (D)

May

5 May

Rhubarb is a bulky, sprawling shrub with high space and nutrient requirements. Now the strong stalks are ripening. These must not be cut off, but twisted out at the base.
If the plant is forced from March onwards, harvesting can even begin up to four weeks earlier. To force the rhubarb's growth, spread mature manure around the young shoots and put a rhubarb pot, a box or a bucket over them, removing it on frost-free days. Since it takes the plant a lot of energy to develop earlier, you should only harvest half of the stalks afterwards.

Notes / Birthdays

In England, these vessels are known as forcers. In the case of rhubarb, they reduce the level of oxalic acid, making the stalks milder and more digestible.
Garden: De Boschhoeve (NL)

May

6 May

With their blossoms in subtle colours and their beautiful sword-shaped leaves which stay attractive throughout the season, bearded irises (formerly *Iris* barbata hybrids) are the darlings of sunswept flower beds and gravel gardens with dry, chalky soil. A practical way to arrange the many different varieties is according to height. The traditional botanical nomenclature is still adhered to in most cases, although it has now been replaced by a more recent one: the dwarf bearded iris (formerly *Iris* barbata nana hybrids), which flowers in April, is now known as Standard Dwarf Bearded (SDB). The 40-to-70-cm-high media hybrids which blossom in May were assigned to the group Intermedia Bearded (IB), whereas the Elatior hybrids with their height of more than 70 cm, which flower from late May onwards, were assigned to the Tall Bearded (TB) types.

The bearded iris 'Pearly Dawn' stands its ground between *Geranium cinereum* 'Ballerina' (background), *Armeria maritima* 'Rubra' and the seed pods of *Pulsatilla vulgaris*.
Garden and design: Peter Janke (D)

May

7 May

If rhododendrons disappoint with withered brown buds instead of flowering, it's the fault of the rhododendron cicada, which is only 0.5 cm long. In September, when it lays its eggs in the inner scales of the young flower buds, it transmits the fungus which causes them to mummify and dry out. Now is the time to remove as many brown buds as you can and spray the remaining buds in the morning if they're heavily infested, as the cicadas, which hatch in May, are still torpid then. In August/September, you should catch the pests by using yellow panel traps before they lay their eggs – or even spray the plants again.

This large-flowered rhododendron looks almost like a bridal bouquet. Its pure white starts to shine in the evening and can even brighten up the shady background of a garden.

May

8 May

Innovative terrace planks look like wood and are robust and easy to maintain. WPC (wood-plastic composite) is the name of the composite made of wood fibres or wood flour and plastic. These thermoplastically treated planks coated with plastic are highly weather- and pest-resistant, non-slip and splinter-free. These are also the features of terrace planks made of plexiglas® wood, a wood-plastic composite made of wood fibres and acrylics. Like WPC planks, they're available in different colours and surface structures – mostly in the easy-to-handle hollow chamber system.

Notes / Birthdays

The cedarwood slats and covering for the ground and terrace function here as a uniform counterweight to the colourful plants.
Garden: Chelsea Flower Show,
design: Adam Frost (GB)

May

9 May

The leaves of cherry laurels, rhododendrons and many other plants often display notched margins – telling signs that the annoying black vine weevils have been feeding on the outer edges of the leaves. Trying to catch the weevils during their nocturnal feeding activities is of little use. It's much more efficient to use nematodes against their larvae, which mainly eat the tender roots. For this to work, the ground will need to have heated up to 15–25°C, which is why April/May and August/September are the best times to do this. You can order the threadworms by post. Mix them into stagnant water in the morning or evening – not in the full sun, as they're sensitive to UV light – and then pour the mixture around the plants affected.

Notes / Birthdays

The more the 60-cm-high parrot tulip 'Fantasy' opens its exotically green-flamed, ragged flowers, the more it loses the typical tulip shape.

May

10 May

The sight of the grapeflower vine *(Wisteria)* opening its fragrant 20–25-cm-long floral clusters in May/June will stop you in your tracks. This poisonous climbing plant with its purple and white flowers does have its peculiarities, though. After a hesitant start, its shoots soon become as thick as an arm, heavy and up to 10 metres long. Since they entwine around the supports, the latter must be solid and provide a lot of space – so rose arches and drainpipes are strictly taboo! The grapeflower looks best on bowers, pergolas and facades, where you can later admire its bean-type seed pods too. Incidentally, *Wisteria floribunda* winds clockwise, whereas *Wisteria sinensis* winds counter-clockwise.

Notes / Birthdays

The Japanese azaleas and the grapeflower vine in this oriental garden are cut back at least three times a season to make them nice and shapely.
Garden: Glaser family (D)

May

11 May

With its richly flowering plants and trees, the merry month of May is also the time when large quantities of pollen are released. This leaves clearly visible yellowish-brown streaks on the surface of ponds and pools. Fish them out of the water using a scoop net, which you should preferably line with fleece. Removing the pollen streaks prevents the water from becoming enriched with nutrients. Incidentally, as soon as your pond has heated up to more than 12°C, you may feed the fish in them again. Any fish that have spent the winter indoors or in the garage can now be put back in the pond.

Notes / Birthdays

A modern aquatic garden planted to bring out the contrasts: topiarised common beeches *(Fagus sylvatica)*, lupins *(Lupinus polyphyllus* 'Chandelier'), globeflowers *(Trollius)* and white laceflowers *(Orlaya grandiflora)*.
Garden: Chelsea Flower Show,
design: Luciano Giubbilei (GB)

May

12 May

We know from our own experience – as well as from weather records – that cold snaps often occur as late as May. Inflows of polar air can cause ground and night frost and severely damage blossoms, seedlings and plants from frost-free regions. It was probably during the Middle Ages that this period, known as Ice Saints, was pinpointed as occurring between 11 and 15 May. As a result of global warming, however, frosty days appear to have become more moderate and to have shifted to an earlier date. To be on the safe side, don't take tropical plants or vegetables that require warm weather outside or plant them out until the second half of May or the end of the month.

Notes / Birthdays

It's nice to have a thrill now and then: the only way to reach this outdoor paradise is via a little gangplank. Optically, the plants, furniture and space-divider are all based on the rectangle.
Garden: Chelsea Flower Show, design: Marcus Barnett (GB)

May

13 May

Elegant and lasting plays of colour in flower beds and herbaceous borders can also be achieved using shrubs or subshrubs with grey and silver foliage. They blend in with all blossom and leaf colours and give the garden structure and a wealth of subtle nuances. What all these plants require most is full sun and permeable soil. Their colour shows that they've adapted to hot sunny locations. This is because silver and grey tones are always the result of fine hairs or wax deposits which protect the leaves and stalks from the wind and the sun.

Notes / Birthdays

This combination of the leaves of *Carex elata* 'Aurea' (gold), *Heuchera* 'Obsidian' (dark red) and *Alchemilla mollis* (green) looks more colourful than many a blossom. Hovering above it all are the white spherical flowers of *Allium* 'Mont Blanc'.
Garden: Chelsea Flower Show, design: Darren Hawkes (GB)

May

14 May

What would Mother's Day be without flowers? Every year it falls on the second Sunday in May, at least in the USA and many other countries, when the garden displays countless blossoms which can be made into very personal bouquets. In the UK, however, it falls on the fourth Sunday in Lent, which means it's usually celebrated in the second half of March or early April. Daffodils, require preparatory treatment before they can be put in a vase with other flowers. Since they secrete a slimy substance which causes the other plants to wither rapidly, it's best to cut into the bottom of the stalks and put them into hot water for a time to close the ends. Lilac is quite different: to ensure it doesn't wither quickly, remove the leaves at the base and cut a cross in the stalks. Then dip the shoots into hot water for two minutes and put them into a vase full of lukewarm water.

The enchanting May green and white of the tulip 'Spring Green' and viburnum twigs from the garden have been combined here with hawthorn and cow-parsley brought home from a May walk.
Garden: Elisabeth Imig and Silke Imig-Gerold (D)

May

15 May

The graceful mono- or polychromatic flowers of columbine *(Aquilegia)* float elfishly above the foliage between May and June. Regarding the shape of their blossoms, long-spurred types (breeds of *Aquilegia caerulea)* can be distinguished from those with short spurs or no spurs at all. These go back to *Aquilegia vulgaris.* Columbine not only repeatedly creates new colour variants by itself, but also spreads by itself through self-seeding. To stop it from running to seed, cut off withered parts in good time. This gives these robust shrubs, which usually only reach an age of four years, a slightly longer life.

Notes / Birthdays

Bumble-bees with a short proboscis or none at all often remove the nectar by biting into blossoms or spurs. Here is the pure white *Aquilegia vulgaris* 'Alba' with its short spur.

May

16 May

The codling moth (also known as "fruit maggot"), is a dreaded pest whose larvae eat through to the core of apples, creating passage-ways and making them look "worm-eaten". From mid-May onwards, the first butterflies hatch and go off in search of a partner at dusk, then lay their eggs on leaves and young fruits shortly after fertilisation. You can often prevent fertilisation by hanging up pheromone traps early enough. The males are attracted by the pheromones in the trap and get stuck to the glue.

Notes / Birthdays

Ornamental onions *(Allium)*, columbines *(Aquilegia)* and forget-me-nots *(Myosotis sylvatica)* contribute to the playful and multicoloured spring goings-on under this apple tree.
Garden: Susanne Paus, Peter Zweil (D)

May

17 May

If your roses have often suffered in the past from fungal infections such as black spot, rose rust and mildew, you should treat them prophylactically with fungicides before the blossom and repeat the procedure two weeks later. However, never spray them when the weather is hot and sunny, and never during the blossom. Most importantly of all, make sure the spray mist wets the undersides of the leaves too. Note: the shoots and leaves of many varieties are still soft after sprouting and react sensitively to chemical pesticides. Put off the treatment for one to two weeks if this is the case.

Notes / Birthdays

A greenhouse embedded in a small kitchen garden is useful in summer too: inside it, vegetables from southerly regions bear especially large quantities of fruit.
Garden: Kristin Lammerting (D)

May

18 May

Heat-loving young plants like tomatoes, zucchinis, cucumbers, celery, aubergines, artichokes, bell peppers and chillies can now be planted out in the open air. These sun worshippers are heavy nutrient feeders, and they provide the best harvests when they find soil rich in nutrients in a warm and sheltered place in bright sunlight. Before planting, fix up a solid support for all plants which need something to hold on to, so as not to damage the root ball.

Notes / Birthdays

The original flower-bed arrangement, the decorative covering of the pathways and the ornamental planting of vegetables, berry vines and herbs make this small, urban fruit and vegetable garden enchantingly decorative.
Garden: Kristin Lammerting (D)

May

19 May

Unwanted green is now spreading by the day. An especially stubborn candidate here is goutweed *(Aegopodium podagraria)*, which reproduces itself by proliferating subterranean runners and through its seeds. If even just a small part of them stays in the ground, the shrub will sprout again quickly. Here are three tried and tested methods to combat it:

- Mulch it "to death". Cover the entire area with cardboard or antiweed fleece and a 10-cm-high layer of mulch for two years.
- Eat it. Remove all the leaves regularly. Like spinach, the young leaves can be prepared raw or steamed in a variety of ways.
- Spray it. Special fully systemic compounds can be sprayed against goutweed when temperatures are 15–25°C. These don't harm bees or other beneficial insects.

The plants, trees and wooden seat in this small designer garden all look very natural. Openings in the ground covering keep the proliferation of the plants in check.
Garden: Chelsea Flower Show, design: Adam Frost (GB)

20 May

The choice of a dogwood should depend on the soil. In slightly acidic soils rich in humus, flowering dogwood *(Cornus florida)* and *Cornus nuttallii* with their different varieties develop into magnificent solitary shrubs. In heavy, loamy soils with a higher pH value, however, they're extremely susceptible to dogwood anthracnose, a fungal infection which is still incurable. By contrast, Chinese *(Cornus kousa* var. *chinensis)* or Japanese *(Cornus kousa* var. *kousa)* dogwood and their varieties are better able to cope with these soils. The Cornus hybrids 'Venus', *Cornus kousa* var. *kousa* and 'Appalachian Spring' *(Cornus florida)* are generally regarded as being fungus-resistant.

Notes / Birthdays

With its white and pink bracts, flowering dogwood *(Cornus florida* – in this case, the 'Rubra' variety) relies on seduction. These bracts are designed to attract insects and then direct them towards the unassuming actual blossoms in the centre.

May

21 May

Unlike large seating and grill areas in which people get together socially, recesses in hedges and free spaces between grasses, shrubs, roses and fruit and vegetable patches or by the pond soon become places of refuge and niches in which to enjoy a sense of well-being. These small areas are intended for private rest and recreation – especially when they allow you to experience the high points of the garden from close quarters. For such places, use spots at the edge of the garden which have previously been neglected, or include a peaceful oasis of this kind when creating a new feature in the garden.

Notes / Birthdays

_____

_____

_____

_____

While sitting on this bench amid the shrubs and bushes and sheltered by a tree, you can use all your senses to enjoy the fragrance and magic of the world of flowers around you.
Garden: Elisabeth Imig and Silke Imig-Gerold (D)

May

22 May

Corten steel is becoming more and more popular as a material for garden design. This weather-resistant structural steel is equally suitable for fountains, privacy screen fences, borderings for flower beds and pathways, supporting walls, braziers, plant receptacles, garden doors and sculptures. Its surface is formed by a layer of rust, which protects the element from further corrosion and requires no maintenance of any kind. With its earthy tones, corten steel blends into the plant world harmoniously, making it suitable for modern and classical gardens alike.

Notes / Birthdays

The eye-catcher in this little urban garden is the fountain made of corten steel – its cubic shape in perfect harmony with the geometrically planted *Allium* 'Purple Sensation' and black mondo grass (*Ophiopogon planiscapus* 'Niger'). *Design: Peter Janke (D)*

May

23 May

When lilac *(Syringa vulgaris)* is in bloom, it transforms the garden into a riot of colour. Over time, however, these robust shrubs will take up a lot of space, reaching a height of 6 metres and 5 metres in width. To make sure they don't take up all the available space – or to enable them to fit into small gardens too – you can raise the crown of these shrubs, which take well to cutting back. This keeps the lower part airy and affords a view into the rear parts of the garden. An additional advantage is that the area around the roots still gets enough light to allow attractive plants to grow beneath it. Shrubs which have become too large can also be restrained by pruning them back strongly. The best time for this is after the blossom.

Notes / Birthdays

The scent of lilac bathes the tone-in-tone flower beds of *Allium* and also lingers in the air above this eye-catching elements in this cottage garden: the column with the planting bowl and the banded sphere, all made of corten steel.
Garden: Elisabeth Imig and Silke Imig-Gerold (D)

May

24 May

Some roses open their blossoms in May already. These include early wild roses (such as *Rosa hugonis* or *Rosa spinosissima)* and park roses like 'Nevada', 'Marguerite Hilling' or the so-called spring varieties (for example 'Frühlingsduft', 'Frühlingsgold', 'Maigold'). These fragrant roses, most of which blossom only once, were created in the 1940s and 1950s by the German breeder Wilhelm Kordes by crossing with Scotch roses *(Rosa spinosissima).* They're all impressive shrubs which also tolerate half-shade and are suitable for romantic or natural-looking gardens.

Notes / Birthdays

At the feet of the rose 'Frühlingsgold', we can see coral spurge *(Euphorbia coralloides),* Lydian broom *(Genista lydia)* and silver-leafed santolina *(Santolina).*
Garden and design: Peter Janke (D)

May

25 May

With their huge and fascinatingly beautiful blossoms, moutan peonies belong to the old plant aristocracy of China, where they were cultivated 2,000 years ago. As slow growers, they're ideal in front of terraces or for sitting areas, courtyards and small or oriental gardens. The Suffruticosa hybrids mainly blossom in white to pink, and Lutea hybrids in yellow to red tones. More recent varieties are the frost-hardy and fungus-resistant Rockii hybrids and the compact intersectional hybrids (also known as Itoh hybrids).

These crosses of tree peonies and herbaceous peonies display herbaceous growth and good winter-hardiness, as well as long-lived blossoms in white, yellow, pink and red reminiscent of those of tree peonies.

Notes / Birthdays

'Copper Kettle' is an intersectional peony which delights with the enchanting yellow, orange and red tones of its semi-filled flowers. These can reach a size of up to 20 cm.

May

26 May

Above the herbaceous borders, the festival season opens with the high species and varieties of ornamental onion *(Allium)* and their spherical blossoms. They need little space and their foliage soon starts to retract. *Allium*, which bloom in May/June, help to bridge the gap between the blossom of the late tulips and daffodils and the flowering of the roses. They include *A. aflatunense* 'Purple Sensation', *A. nigrum* or the varieties 'Lucy Ball' and 'Mount Everest'. On the other hand, *Allium* which bloom in June/July – such as *A. christophii, A. atropurpureum, A. sphaerocephalon* and varieties like 'Globemaster', 'Ambassador', 'Forelock', 'Mercurius' or 'Beau Regard' – are colourful companions for roses and early blooming shrubs.

Notes / Birthdays

Performing an intermezzo of lilac tones are the late-blooming parrot tulip 'Blue Parrot' and the Persian onion *(Allium* 'Purple Sensation').
Garden: Elisabeth Imig and Silke Imig-Gerold (D)

May

27 May

Siberian bugloss *(Brunnera macrophylla)* is a guarantee for picturesque effects in half-shade or shade – thanks not only to its blue and white blossoms reminiscent of forget-me-nots, but also to its beautiful heart-shaped leaves, which sprout early and retract late. Varieties with a white and green leaf pattern, in particular, brighten up dark spots in herbaceous borders. The most decorative of these include 'Jack Frost', with its green veins on a silvery white background and its blue blossoms, and 'Mr. Morse', which has similar leaves but white blossoms. However, lively accents are also set by 'Langtrees' (speckled in silver) and 'Silver Wings' (with silver patches).

Notes / Birthdays

White Japanese primrose *(Primula japonica* 'Alba'), wood forget-me-nots *(Myosotis sylvatica)* and chestnut-leaved rodgersia *(Rodgersia aesculifolia)* make a good team for places in half-shade which are not too dry.
Garden and design: Peter Janke (D)

May

28 May

Time and time again, spreading trees and shrubs at plot boundaries lead to disputes between neighbours. Trellis hedges provide an elegant solution for green visual cover without overhanging branches. They don't totally overshadow the garden and leave enough space to plant below them.

A single trellis tree can close gaps, while planting a row of trees even allows you to raise walls and prevent people from looking into the garden from above. Large trellis hedges are often created from small-leaved lime trees *(Tilia cordata)* and London plane trees *(Platanus × hispanica)*. Topiariable trees and shrubs with a magnificent autumn colouring – such as field maple *(Acer campestre)*, common hornbeam *(Carpinus betulus)* or common beech *(Fagus sylvatica)* – are recommended for small gardens.

Notes / Birthdays

A narrow wall offers a modern sunken garden a degree of privacy. Complementing it here is a trellis hedge made of field maple *(Acer campestre)*.
Garden: Chelsea Flower Show, design: Marcus Barnett (GB)

May

29 May

To make sure there's a rich berry harvest, currants, gooseberries and other berries should be kept evenly moist. The strawberries are already starting to blossom and fructify, so now, at the latest, is the time to remove the fleeces that were used to protect them and precipitate their growth.

This must be done if pollinators are to be able to reach the blossoms unhindered. At the same time, protect the ripening fruits from ground moisture and contamination by laying straw, rough wood or polystyrene wool under the plants. This keeps them clean and prevents fungal infections such as grey mould.

This trio of common bistort *(Persicaria bistorta* 'Superba', also *Bistorta officinalis)*, ornamental onion *(Allium* 'Purple Sensation') and Siberian iris *(Iris sibirica)* fares especially well at the edge of a pond or in slightly moist earth.
Garden: Susanne Paus, Peter Zweil (D)

May

30 May

Proliferating water lilies which spread their leaves over each other or over the entire surface of the water last summer should now be rejuvenated. If they're growing in mesh baskets, cut off the old parts of the rhizome at the rear, close the cut using active charcoal and let it dry for a short while. Then reline the mesh basket with a new planting fleece, fill the basket with dampened pond earth until it's three quarters full and plant the rhizome horizontally or at a slight angle so that it's high enough to just cover the tip of the vegetation. Finally, carefully fold the ends of the planting fleece over one another and weigh them down with pebbles or a stone.

Notes / Birthdays

Large landscaped gardens have a lot to gain from generous planting. Here, the yellow iris *(Iris pseudacorus)* has been allowed to take possession of the water-filled ditch with its rhizomes.
Garden: Kasteel Oostkerke (B)

May

31 May

Small gardens, in particular, have a lot to gain from multifunctional elements, that is to say, when they can be used in a variety of ways. The pavilion on the right is a good example of this. Its back wall is a privacy screen which combines a burbling wall fountain with a practical place in which to keep things. What's more, the wall and the stone benches store heat and keep cool air away. Providing a garden element with multiple functions is always a challenge for one's creativity and designing ability – and it usually helps to save a good deal of space.

Notes / Birthdays

This pavilion owes its uniform appearance to only two materials: the yellowish sandstone of the privacy wall and benches and the wood of the pergola and garden furniture.
Garden: Chelsea Flower Show,
design: Adam Frost (GB)

May

1 June

Rose archways not only provide support for the plants but are also eye-catching and can be used to partition space, if they're the appropriate size, material and style for the garden. This also helps them to fit into the garden in winter when the plants are bare. Choose as wide an arch as possible. Roses bloom more abundantly when their tendrils are not vertical but are guided horizontally in gentle spirals.

Rose archways need a space where they can fulfil a design-based function, for example over a pathway or marking a visual axis. The area framed by the arch should also be focused on a highlight behind it.

Notes / Birthdays

Who wouldn't want to step through this fragrant rose archway and take a seat on the woven willow bench to catch the fragrant scents in the air?
Garden: Nina Balthau (B)

June

2 June

Roses and clematis are a great team for rose archways, pergolas, trellises, summer houses and obelisks. With a low-growing clematis, you can even help the bare lower area of many climbing plants and ramblers to new splendour. Even when the rose is already established, you can plant clematis next to it. However, it should be planted 30–50 cm away and with a root barrier between it and the rose. The root ball must be planted deeply enough so that the lower two pairs of shoots are under the earth. To prevent them from being bent or broken, the clematis shoots are led to the support or the rose with the aid of poles.

A liaison between the fragrant rambler 'Guirlande d'Amour' and the abundantly blooming Clematis viticella will bear blossoms until September.

June

3 June

On hot summer days, birds also need more liquids and are grateful for drinking and bathing places. These should be no deeper than 2.5–10 cm and should be shallow at the outsides. Place them in highly visible areas, that is to say away from bushes and shrubs where danger could be lurking. A decorative bird-bath in the middle of a flower bed, a stone fountain with a gentle trough and a rough surface, or bird-baths to hang in trees will quickly attract thirsty birds. On hot days, the bird-baths should be thoroughly cleaned every day before being refilled with fresh water.

Notes / Birthdays

The colour and shape of the pergola with its solid pinewood beams are continued in the screening walls, transforming this modern city garden into an outside room.
Garden: Chelsea Flower Show,
design: Nicole Fischer, Daniel Auderset (CH)

June

4 June

Right in the middle of summery temperatures and before summer officially begins on 21 June, there is often a significant drop in temperatures in central Europe between 4 and 20 June (usually around 11 June) – frequently accompanied by rain (or even snow in Alpine regions). This period is known as "sheep's cold" because in the past, sheep were shorn around this time. In central Europe, shearing was postponed until the end of June because of the cold. Vegetables which need warmth, such as tomatoes, aubergines and paprika, should be protected with fleece or tomato covers during this period.

Notes / Birthdays

A flower bed in front of a terrace can accentuate even the most beautiful views of the landscape with seasonal colours all year round.
Garden: Emy and Peter Ultee (NL), design: In Goede Aarde (NL)

June

5 June

Whether they're among roses and larkspur, the fragrant yellow-green clouds of lady's mantle *(Alchemilla mollis)* look almost magical in a flower bed with sage and geranium or as a long-lasting decoration in a vase. But did you know that this robust shrub also has uses in the kitchen in addition to its diverse medicinal effects?

When harvested during the flowering period, the young leaves can be added raw to salads, dips and smoothies, steamed like spinach or dried and brewed as a tea. After flowering, lady's mantle can be pruned close to the ground. This prevents the seeds from spreading and encourages the shrub to yield attractive, compact thickets.

Notes / Birthdays

This square makes the most of different shapes in peaceful shades of green. Between sculpted hedges and balls, the lady's mantle is allowed to flourish informally.
Garden: Ria Lengton (NL)

June

6 June

With their green, yellowy or blue-green foliage, which can also have decorative white and yellow edges or markings, hostas (also known as blue day lilies) are among the most attractive foliage plants. They shine in shady flower beds and around ponds, in front of and beneath shrubs, whose root pressure doesn't bother them, but also grow well in pots – for example, around a north-facing building entrance, or flanking a shady bench, or to enliven a poorly lit courtyard. Depending on the variety, the lily-like white or purple blossoms appear under the leaves from June or later. Their only disadvantage is that snails find them irresistible too!

Notes / Birthdays

The hosta ensemble in this shady courtyard is accompanied by palmate maple *(Acer palmatum)* and frost-sensitive potted plants such as houseleek trees *(Aeonium arboreum)* and society garlic *(Tulbaghia violacea,* left).
Garden: t'Hof Overwellingen (NL)

June

7 June

When the roses begin to blossom, rose chafers also appear and feed on the petals and stamens of the flowers. These pretty beetles with their shimmering green metallic wing cases are particularly fond of scented rose varieties. However, declaring war on them is prohibited, as they're a protected species. Their larvae are even beneficial to the ecosystem. They look similar to cock chafer or summer chafer grubs and are often found in rotten tree stumps or when turning compost heaps. But unlike these grubs, the rose chafer larvae eat rotten plants rather than roots, thus contributing to the formation of humus.

Notes / Birthdays

This flower bed shines in a proven three-colour combination when the roses are in blossom: pink and red (roses), blue and blue-violet (larkspur, sage) and white (summer marguerite)
. *Garden: Elisabeth Imig and Silke Imig-Gerold (D)*

June

8 June

Karl Foerster called the delphinium "the rose's special favourite" – it would probably already be our favourite, too, if it were less often a disappointment, with its short lifespan and refusal to bloom once more in autumn. These problems apply mostly to the imposing pacific hybrids, with their large blossoms. The varieties from the Elatum and Belladonna groups are, on the contrary, long lasting, as are varieties from the new millennium series. Belladonna varieties in particular blossom again reliably in September/October, if they are cut back to a height of 10 cm after 20 June, provided with a fast-acting mineral fertiliser, kept evenly moist and have their delicate new shoots carefully protected from snails.

Notes / Birthdays

Delphinium varieties bloom in gorgeous shades of blue, violet and pink, as well as white. Here, a Delphinium pacific hybrid in an iridescent blue-violet with a white centre.

June

9 June

Many gardeners avoid sunny yellow and orange-yellow, as these colours disturb the harmony of a cool-toned planting. However, this doesn't apply to sulphur yellow, which can be lightened and "cooled" by white. How lucky for cool-toned combinations that there are increasing numbers of pale yellow varieties available! Some examples: yarrow *(Achillea filipendulina* 'Hella Glashoff'), dyer's chamomile *(Anthemis tinctoria* 'Sauce Hollandaise'), Arctic daisy *(Arctanthemum arcticum* 'Schwefelglanz'), thread-leaf coreopsis *(Coreopsis* 'Crème Brûlée', *Coreopsis verticillata* 'Moonbeam'), black samson *(Echinacea purpurea* 'Sunrise') and many varieties of iris and day lilies *(Hemerocallis).*

Notes / Birthdays

Wonderfully matched with the blue and violet of delphinium and lavender, dusky pink *(Centranthus)* and white of this double border are the pale yellow Turkish sage *(Phlomis russeliana),* the creamy yellow rose and the yellow-green lady's mantle *(Alchemilla mollis).*

Garden: Cisca and Ireen Schmid (NL)

June

10 June

An important term in garden architecture is "Belvedere" (or "Bellevue"), which refers to an area of high ground with a beautiful view. The term is also used for the structures built on these areas. In large landscaped gardens, an artificial hill is often constructed for this purpose. Although the design and style of the belvedere can be very varied, it always has extremely attractive architecture. These elevated pergolas, pavilions, platforms, temples or rustic log cabins are intended to be eye-catching in their own right from other perspectives. Like the pavilion on the right, which is a cosy water resort and an idyllic backdrop simultaneously.

Notes / Birthdays

With its reflections and stimulating atmosphere, water has always been a source of fascination. As in classic precedents, this rural garden doesn't miss the opportunity to crown the watercourse with a pavilion.
Garden: Nina Balthau (B)

June

11 June

Warmth and sunshine are drawing vegetable plants out of the ground at the moment. Some of them need to be earthed up as soon as they reach heights of 10–15 cm. This encourages the formation of tubers such as potatoes and Jerusalem artichokes. The plants should be earthed up twice more in the following weeks so that the tubers develop well.

The delicate shoots of peas and beans, but also as headed cabbage, pepper, cucumber and tomato plants, benefit from the more stable standing provided by earthing up. It also facilitates root development and thus encourages growth and yield.

Notes / Birthdays

Although stairway greenery is usually planted along gaps, here the boxwood hebe *(Hebe buxifolia)* thrives under and between sandstone steps, which are fixed into the outer supporting walls

Garden: Chelsea Flower Show,
design: Charlie Albone (AUS)

June

12 June

A tree in front of the terrace has many advantages: its wide crown is a picturesque sunshade and privacy screen at the same time, preventing views from above. A deciduous tree with a variety of seasonal highlights enriches outdoor life with atmospheric charm and allows you to experience the seasons close up. And last but not least, a tree in front of the terrace opens up the third dimension, so that the garden isn't only experienced as an area but as a three-dimensional space. When choosing your tree, take into account the fact that the house tree will become a part of the family, whose size or growth shouldn't disturb the proportions of the house or garden, even years later.

Notes / Birthdays

The Chinese dogwood *(Cornus kousa* var. *chinensis)* is a magnificent house tree. It shines with white bracts in June, afterwards with strawberry-like fruits, and in autumn with red foliage.
Garden: private garden, Düsseldorf (D)

June

13 June

Mild nights with glow-worms sending out their characteristic light signals like Morse code are the epitome of romantic summer nights. Did you know that you are witnessing a scientific singularity? While a standard light bulb emits 5 per cent of its energy as light, these unprepossessing beetles manage to transform 95 per cent of their self-generated energy into light (bioluminescence). In the process, the worm-like wingless females transmit their declarations of love into the night from elevated positions, while the males take flashing flights searching for them. After mating, the love light is extinguished, along with the life of these wonderful creatures.

Notes / Birthdays

Entrances and driveways should always be attractive, as they act like a visiting card. These flower beds with the small shrub roses 'Lavender Dream', *Geranium* 'Rozanne' and *Salvia* 'Blauhügel' fulfil this task with blossoms until the first frost.
Garden: Paul Vandenberghe (B)

June

14 June

Rose gardens are based on the idea of paying homage to the beauty of a single plant. They first appeared in the eighteenth century, as the range of rose varieties, until then limited to 20 garden roses and a number of wild roses, shot up thanks to the discovery of artificial fertilisation. Rose fans still like to present their charges in the classical fashion today. Box and other evergreen shrubs are used as surrounds and shaped accents. As geometric features, they bring tranquillity to the free, irregular growth of the roses, cover up their often bare bases and, with their uniform green, help the beautiful blossoms to put on a glamorous show.

Notes / Birthdays

A sweet fragrance rests over this classic rose garden, which is given three-dimensionality by highlights such as a sundial, round trees and an obelisk with clematis.
Garden: t'Hof Overwellingen (NL)

June

15 June

Sometimes you only need to wait until June to meet a new garden treasure: a blossoming rose that you fall for right away. No problem, since roses in containers are now available. As they already form fine roots in the pot, they can be planted all the year round, unless the ground is frozen. They're rather more expensive than other types, but have the advantage that the colour and shape of their blossoms can already be seen. Before planting, these roses need to be watered well. Then the pot is removed and the plants planted such that the graft is approximately 5 cm under the surface.

Notes / Birthdays

The tête-à-tête of the purple-pink striped bourbon rose 'Honorine de Brabant' and the 1.2-metre-high shrub rose 'Ballerina' are subtly balanced.

June

16 June

Rambler roses are in! With their vigorously growing, flexible shoots, they can extensively cover trees, walls and pergolas. Most of them bloom only once, but remarkably prolifically and over a period of several weeks. And although the blossoms are often very small, they do appear in larger clusters.

Growers have now developed a new generation of rambler varieties. These are suited to archways, trellis and obelisks, thanks to their moderate growth (up to roughly 3 metres tall). They often bloom in the rare rambler colours of yellow, red or pink and are even beautifully scented. This means it's definitely worthwhile studying rose catalogues!

Notes / Birthdays

The fragrant blossoms of 'Félicité et Perpétue' open from pink buds to form full white tufts. The old-fashioned single blooming rambler rose grows to a height of 5 metres.

June

17 June

If you're searching for a rose arbour or want to sit on a bench surrounded by roses, you should take four points into account when choosing, to maximise your enjoyment:
- Choose the right size of climbing or rambler rose! Don't pick a fast-growing variety if the shoots are only intended to cover the arch above a bench.
- Choose a fragrant variety.
- Choose a variety which has as few thorns as possible, or none at all, to avoid injury.
- Choose a repeat-blooming variety, or one which at least flowers once more in late summer.

Notes / Birthdays

Many vigorous shrub roses can be led up climbing supports. Here, the repeat-flowering 'Bonanza', which grows up to 1.8 metres tall, envelops the metal pergola in red-gold splendour.
Garden: Elisabeth Imig and Silke Imig-Gerold (D)

June

18 June

As the summer slowly reaches its peak, warmth-loving fruiting vegetables such as tomatoes, peppers, aubergines and pumpkins shouldn't be allowed to dry out – but neither should they be kept too wet, so that the young plants are then forced to put down deeper roots, allowing them to find more nutrients and grow more robustly. To ensure that tomatoes and co. aren't in for a shock, they should be provided with water at the correct temperature. To do this, fill several watering cans in the morning, so that the water has time to warm up before you water the plans in the evening. Important note: to avoid fungal diseases, never water the leaves!

Notes / Birthdays

On hot days, water barrels and watering cans are vital. The signs of wear on the zinc containers are unmissable and lend the still life a nostalgic flair.
Garden: Hennie Menken (NL)

June

19 June

Classic herbaceous borders need plenty of sun and are fascinating thanks to their picturesque combinations of blossoms and ornamental foliage. Mixed borders impress with even more variety when they include roses and shrubs. The more subtly these beds are planted, the more serene the pathway and its surface appear. In order to develop their magnificent charm, borders should be at least 2 metres wide and 5 metres long. You can also integrate passages and stepping stones (laid at step width), to allow access for planting and maintenance.

For double borders, the effect is enhanced when the colours are similar. Lupins, geraniums, white astrantia and delphiniums are combined in this mixed border, as well as with roses and hydrangeas in cool tones.
Garden: Elisabeth Imig and Silke Imig-Gerold (D)

June

20 June

The terms "roofscaped tree" or "umbrella tree" are not names for trees, but describe a shape which can be created using several deciduous trees. This process requires shaping the crown into a horizontal roof of leaves over the course of years with the help of a stable framework in order to create an atmospheric source of shade. Established "umbrella trees" can be purchased in many tree nurseries. The best-suited trees are those which take well to pruning, such as sweet buckeye *(Aesculus flava)*, common hornbeam *(Carpinus betulus)*, common beech *(Fagus sylvatica)*, maidenhair tree *(Ginkgo biloba)*, London plane *(Platanus × hispanica)*, pin oak *(Quercus palustris)* and common lime *(Tilia × vulgaris)*.

Umbrella trees *(Tilia* x *vulgaris)* in a pergola shape provide this seating area with shade and a sense of security. The marble water wall in the background offers a refreshing contrast.
Garden: RHS Chelsea Flower Show, design: del Buono/Gazerwitz, Landscape Architecture (GB)

June

21 June

Herbs not only lend meals their aroma and sophistication, but can also ward off diseases and pests from neighbouring plants. If you plant the herbs with the appropriate partner, you can use their valuable properties dually right away:
- Lavender drives aphids and ants away from roses.
- Summer savory keeps black bean aphids away from beans.
- Wormwood prevents white pine blister rust in redcurrants.
- Garlic wards off fungal diseases in strawberries and roses.
- Nasturtium keeps woolly apple aphids away from fruit trees.

A love of gardens is manifested here in a trio: while vegetables ripen protected by a fence, roses (left) and herbs (right) romp in the wicker-fenced gardens.
Garden: Ilka Dorn (D)

June

22 June

June is the "berry month", in which not only strawberries but also redcurrants, gooseberries and blueberries ripen. However, not all of them require a large amount of garden space. So-called "hanging strawberries" and "climbing strawberries" grow beautifully even in hanging baskets, boxes and flowerpots. There, they grow runners up to 1.5 metres long over the course of the season, which also bloom and bear delicious fruits up until autumn. But climbing strawberries cannot truly climb. Their shoots must be tied up, for example to trellises, climbing supports, obelisks or balcony railings.

And to allow them to best perform their yearly programme, they should be pampered with strawberry fertiliser every 14 days until August.

Notes / Birthdays

_____

_____

_____

_____

Sun-warmed from the flower bed, strawberries taste as if they come from paradise. However, they only develop their full-flavoured aroma when provided with even soil moisture and full sunlight.
Garden: Elisabeth Imig and Silke Imig-Gerold (D)

June

23 June

Benches are a successful model of comfort, which can also provide the garden with an additional charming element. Here are the four most important design aspects:

- Choose the location so that new views of the house, garden or particular highlights in the garden are opened up.
- The bench should fulfil our archaic need for rear cover. Hedges, planting groups, walls, fences, trellises and many more features can provide protection from behind.
- Benches gain a cosy flair when they're also embedded in green at the sides.
- Finally, the bench itself should be comfortable and visually attractive.

Notes / Birthdays

The bench is brought to life perfectly by its evergreen surroundings. It's embedded in yew hedges, while round-leaved wintergreen trees flank it like guardians.

Garden: Sarina Meijer (NL),
design: A. J. van der Horst (NL)

June

24 June

St John's Day is an important deadline for agriculture and forestry, as well as for gardeners. From St John's Day onwards, herbs are particularly rich in substance. Oak, European beech and maple often start a second budding, the so-called Lammas shoot, which compensates for prior losses from frost and pests. But above all, asparagus and rhubarb are no longer harvested from now on. The perennial plants must gather their strength for the following year, and furthermore, the levels of harmful oxalic acid in rhubarb increase sharply. Both plants should now be given an organic mineral fertiliser to assist them.

Notes / Birthdays

The smoke tree *(Cotinus coggygria* 'Young Lady'), round-headed garlic *(Allium sphaerocephalon)* and alternate-leaved butterfly bush *(Buddleja alternifolia)* fascinate with their contrasting blossom forms and unusual play of colours.
Garden and design: Peter Janke (D)

June

25 June

Towards the end of this month, grasses slow down their growth. Up until this point, the lawn should be mowed twice a week. This supplies plenty of nitrogen-rich cuttings, which are much too valuable to be thrown away.

Spread them on vegetable beds, under trees and shrubs as a fine mulch layer. The remaining cuttings can be thinly spread in secluded areas and left to dry. These dried cuttings can be composted if mixed with coarser garden waste.

However, fresh grass cuttings are off-limits for compost. They stick together to form airtight mats, preventing the composting process and leading to rotting.

Notes / Birthdays

These willow sculptures flicker out of the earth like flames. As nature art, they frame the silver foliage of the round flower bed and also prove themselves as an artful partition.
Garden and design: Peter Janke (D)

June

26 June

Although roses are sun-lovers, many of them don't like hot locations in the full heat of the midday sun. All roses tend to fade faster in these locations. However, if a sunny south-facing spot is the only one available, a heat-resistant variety should be chosen. White roses and small-leaved varieties (such as ground-cover roses) are particularly heat-resistant. Those who wish to plant a dark red or carmine red rose should choose a variety which doesn't turn blue in full sun. Scarlet and coral-coloured roses are little affected.

Notes / Birthdays

From June to July, the tall, imposing flower clusters of foxtail lilies *(Eremurus)* outshine their neighbours. Requirements: full sun and permeable dry ground.
Garden and design: Peter Janke (D)

June

27 June

Redcurrants are among the most robust berries and can fit into even the smallest garden. A pollinating variety isn't necessary, although the berries have better yield in company. The broad shrubs can be used as a hedge along a garden fence or as a partition. Varieties which are grafted onto stems of the buffalo currant *(Ribes aureum)* are real space savers and look delightful when their crowns bear plenty of fruit above flower beds and vegetable beds. Redcurrants can even be grown in the shape of a fan up a trellis with three base shoots each, either up a wall or free-standing.

Notes / Birthdays

_____

_____

_____

_____

Whitecurrants taste milder and are less acidic than redcurrants. To prevent ripening berries from falling victim to birds, they must be protected with nets which reach down to the ground or are tied together under the crown.

June

28 June

Pergolas with a single strut are rarely seen, although they offer a wide range of design possibilities. They can move through the garden as partitions and define different areas. They refine fences and garden boundaries with a picturesque touch, and provide an airy privacy screen with their colonnades. They also allow rose fans to present their favourites without taking up too much floor space. Since they don't provide too much shade, they can also serve as the romantic backdrop for a border or heighten a peaceful lawn area at their base with the impact of their blossoms.

Notes / Birthdays

Full of picturesque buoyancy, fragrant rambler roses such as 'Phyllis Bide' (left), 'Pink Perpétué' (centre) and 'Tausend-schön' (right) welcome visitors to the single-strutted pergola.
Garden: De Zeeuwse Rozentuin (NL)

June

29 June

A succession of warm days and hot spells necessitate ever more frequent watering of lawns and plants. To avoid sunburn, this should be done in the early morning or evening. If the garden hose is pulled through the green refuge for watering, it's likely to take short cuts at border curves and force plants into the flower bed. To avoid this, place hose holders at prominent points. These steer the hose into the right track and keep it away from flower beds.

Notes / Birthdays

Herbs show their best side in formal structures. This herb garden is enlivened by a thyme circle with a rippling fountain. Behind it is a yew arch with a rod of Asclepius, the symbol of the healing professions,

Garden: Chelsea Flower Show,
design: Jekka McVicar
sculpture: Susan Bacon (GB)

June

30 June

As soon as repeat-flowering roses have faded, regular pruning encourages them to form new shoots and blossoms:
- The faded side shoots need to be pruned from repeat-flowering climbing and shrub roses.
- For flower-bed roses, the faded cluster should be trimmed.
- For tea roses, the individual shoots are pruned. The cut surface should be 0.5 cm diagonally above the first complete leaf below it. In the leaf axils, the bud is often already clearly visible. If the shears are used lower down, the plant often needs more strength and time to bloom again.

Notes / Birthdays

For many gardeners, nurseries are among the best places for inspirational encounters and help to make up for some failures in the garden.
Garden and design: Peter Janke (D)

June

1 July

An abundance of summer scents is maturing in garden herbs at the moment. Their flavours are usually most intensive shortly before they bloom. This is the point at which they should be harvested – the best time is in the morning, after the dew has dried. If not used freshly picked, most of them can be frozen. Many also keep their flavour if hung to dry in an airy, shaded place.

Perennial herbs, such as bay, rosemary, lavender, sage, mint, melissa, oregano, marjoram and thyme, can be easily propagated now using stem cuttings.

Notes / Birthdays

This picturesque herb garden in its box frame is outshone by the blood red of the cascading rose 'Super Excelsa'. A scenic feast for the eyes and a magnet for many insects at the same time.

Garden: Winkler family (D)

July

2 July

Whether it's a close-to-nature pond or a formal basin – water draws attention just like a shimmering mirror. That makes it even more disappointing when water lilies fail to bloom. Below is a checklist of the most frequent causes:

- Does the variety have the appropriate water-level height?
- Is the water lily in the full sun? If not, move the plant pot to a sunny spot.
- Has the plant pot become too small? If so, repot the rhizome to a larger container.
- Is the water still? Water lilies don't like fountains or water features.
- Are the buds dying back too soon? This is often due to cold spells during the growth period. However, the plants will recover and bloom later.

Notes / Birthdays

As in this formal pool, a maximum of a third of water surfaces should be covered with floating plants. This allows visitors to also enjoy the attractive reflections of the sky and surroundings.
Garden and design: Stijn Cornilly (B)

July

3 July

Now is the time to sow biennial flowers. It is, of course, possible to buy many plantlets from nurseries and garden centres. Others are available more rarely, for example hollyhock *(Alcea rosea)*, common foxglove *(Digitalis purpurea)*, Canterbury bells *(Campanula medium)* and biennial clary sage *(Salvia sclarea)*. And if you want particular varieties or colours, you'll need to take matters into your own hands here too. A frame isn't required for the purpose.

It's advisable to sow the future garden treasures individually into peat pots and cultivate them there until they're planted out in autumn.

Notes / Birthdays

Red borders are also known as "hot borders". This exotic ensemble is comprised (from l. to r.) of: African millet *(Pennisetum glaucum* 'Purple Majesty'), canna lily *(Canna)*, purple amaranth *(Amaranthus cruentus* 'Velvet Curtains') and brilliant lobelia *(Lobelia fulgens)*. Garden: Hermannshof (D)

July

4 July

The brilliant blossoms of ornamental and kitchen gardens are now ablaze with colour. Did you know that many of them are edible? Alongside bee balm and giant hyssop (on the right of the picture), nasturtium, marigold, some varieties of border of gold, sunflowers, day lilies, roses, dahlias, cornflowers, mallow, aster and poppy are also good to eat. And the blossoms of herbs such as borage, lavender or chives can be used, too, to spice up vinegar and oil, soups, sauces, butter, dips, quark, salads, desserts and cakes. Before using them in the kitchen, make sure that the plants you choose aren't poisonous and avoid using treated or bought flowers.

Notes / Birthdays

A tiered border of Himalayan knotweed *(Aconogonon polystachyum* 'Johanniswolke') and boneset *(Eupatorium)*, bee balm *(Monarda* 'Gewitterwolke'), black samson *(Echinacea purpurea)*, giant hyssop *(Agastache* 'Black Adder') and yarrow *(Achillea* 'Pretty Belinda').
Garden: Maurice Vergote (B)

July

5 July

Many of today's roses are grafted onto a base of *Rosa laxa*, which produces very few shoots in the wild. However, the pale green shoots of the wild rose base frequently break through suddenly next to a rose variety. The wild shoots, or suckers, can mostly be easily recognised by their smaller, heavily feathered foliage. As soon as they appear, the roots should be exposed back to the growth point of the sucker, which should then be torn off all at once from the base from top to bottom. If the sucker is simply pruned at ground level, it will sprout more strongly and deprive the rose of its strength.

Notes / Birthdays

Box borders provide this classic rose garden with a peaceful, evergreen frame, which covers the often sparse or bare base of the rose plants.
Garden: Kasteel Wijlre (NL)

July

6 July

Hollyhocks *(Alcea rosea)*, the biennial, long-legged favourite of farm and cottage gardens, draw plenty of attention between July and September. As if aware of their effect, they're quite demanding. They're only spared from hollyhock rust when they grow in loose soil rich in humus in a sunny, warm spot. Aside from the 2.5-metre-tall varieties which are often planted in the protection of buildings, walls or fences, so that wind and weather cannot affect them, there are also lower, stable varieties, such as 'Majorette' (60–90 cm tall) with half-filled blossoms.

Notes / Birthdays

The Antwerp or fig-leaved hollyhock *(Alcea ficifolia)* is also biennial, but less prone to hollyhock rust than *Alcea rosea*. Like the hollyhock, the plant is also popular with bees and butterflies.
Garden: Elisabeth Imig and Silke Imig-Gerold (D)

July

7 July

Many gardeners are frustrated by the appetite of snails, which spare neither vegetables nor many shrubs. Some exasperated gardeners have even been known to throw the snails into their neighbour's garden or nearby meadows. Don't do that! The snails are sure to come back. British researchers have discovered that the invertebrates' homing sense only fails them when they're thrown more than 20 metres. Above all, you shouldn't harm the Roman snail, or escargot – for there's a good reason why they're a protected species. With their fondness for wilted leaves and slug eggs, they deserve their place in the garden.

Notes / Birthdays

Those who would like to take up arms against snails are best advised to use plants that snails dislike, such as betony *(Stachys officinalis* 'Hummelo', 'Nivea', 'Rosea'), fennel *(Foeniculum vulgare* 'Giant Bronze') and autumn moor-grass *(Sesleria autumnalis)*.

Garden: Anja and Piet Oudolf, design: Piet Oudolf (NL)

July

8 July

Outdoor furniture is becoming more and more versatile and luxurious. An outdoor kitchen fits this trend. Whether it's self-built, expanded step by step or represents the height of modern expertise, four criteria should be met:
- A floor covering which can support heavy appliances and will not absorb splashes of fat.
- Roofing to protect from the rain.
- Lighting so that the kitchen can be used until late in the evening.
- Running water for cooking and cleaning. Those who also want to cook outside in the wintertime should ensure that the water pipes are frostproof.

Notes / Birthdays

_____

_____

_____

_____

Some people find that it helps their yearning for faraway places if the garden exudes Mediterranean flair. Here, the seating area and outdoor kitchen invite visitors to cook and enjoy food together.
Design: Son Muda Gardens, Majorca (E)

July

9 July

It isn't worth gathering the seeds of every garden plant. Heirloom varieties of sunflower germinate particularly reliably. It's possible to grow plants from them which exhibit the same characteristics as their parent plants. The descendants of varieties which aren't true to seed can take gardeners by surprise with new characteristics. Seeds from F_1 hybrids, on the other hand, don't prove very successful. Those wishing to give it a try should harvest the seeds in sunny, dry weather and store them in labelled envelopes, bags, boxes or jars in a cool, dark place.

Notes / Birthdays

Annual plants bloom across the entire flower bed at this time, giving them their full beauty. Here, we see zinnias, Argentinian vervain *(Verbena bonariensis)*, brilliant lobelia *(Lobelia fulgens)* and African feather grass *(Pennisetum macrourum* 'White Lancer'). *Garden: Hermannshof (D)*

July

10 July

The stone fruits of the sweet cherry are ripe now and deliciously juicy. Sweet cherries are divided into two categories: heart cherries with staining juice and white heart cherries with light-coloured juice, with stones which come loose easily. Sweet cherries usually need a second pollinator. The few self-pollinating varieties don't usually bear as much fruit. If space is an issue, you can get by with two slender column cherry trees or a duo cherry, where two matching pollinating varieties are grafted onto one trunk. When harvesting the fruit, only unsplit, fully ripe fruit should be placed into the basket with their stalks, as these keep longer. All the rest must be used immediately.

Notes / Birthdays

Dense cushions of border of gold *(Tagetes tenuifolia* 'Lemon Gem' and 'Orange Gem') ward off soil worms in this kitchen garden, as well as enhancing meals with their lemon and mandarin flavours.
Garden: De Boschhoeve (NL)

July

11 July

On hot days, it's not only birds, but also cats, hedgehogs, mice, squirrels and other small animals who suffer from thirst. In their search for water, pools with steep walls and water barrels sadly often prove fatal. Water barrels should therefore be covered with lids; this also ensures that less dust gets into the water. In a pool, put a stable wooden board, plank or ladder at a slope in the water. Such a ramp helps to save animals from a harrowing death by drowning. Floating pieces of wood or polystyrene aren't suitable, as the animals are unable to climb onto them.

Notes / Birthdays

Spotlights directed upwards from below can create dramatic garden images. Here, they're used to full effect to draw attention to white birch trunks and the garden background.
Garden: Landesgartenschau Zülpich, design: GartenLandschaft Berg (D)

July

12 July

Zucchini plants blossom and fruit simultaneously. If you wonder why their plants bloom
abundantly but bear very few fruits, you should
know that every plant bears male and female
blossoms, only the female of which yield fruit.
Female blossoms are larger and have an ovary
beneath the petals. If you face the likelihood
of a zucchini glut, you can harvest the flowers
and fill them or fry them. The fruit itself tastes
best when it's 15–20 cm long.
By the way: silvery spots on the zucchini leaves
which cannot be wiped off are not mildew –
these are typical for some varieties.

Notes / Birthdays

The shoots of the calabash cucumber
(*Lagenaria siceraria*) can reach a length of
up to 10 metres on trellises. Aside from
being edible, the range of shapes and sizes
also makes the fruits suitable for use as
containers and musical instruments.
Garden: De Boschhoeve (NL)

July

13 July

Old fruit trees which no longer bear much fruit can undergo a picturesque comeback with the aid of a rambler rose trailing through them. You can now also plant a rambler next to deeply rooted conifers such as larch and pine trees. The best way for them to succeed is to protect them from the root pressure of the trees by planting them 60 cm from the trunk in an open-base pot. The dug-out soil is then generously mixed with compost to improve it. Finally, the rose is tied to the trunk of the tree and its shoots led up into the branches.

Notes / Birthdays

_____

_____

_____

_____

With their exuberant and sumptuous white flowers, the reliable rambler classics 'Bobby James' and 'Lykkefund' cover old fruit trees in this rural garden area.
Garden: Waltham Place (GB)

July

14 July

When the rhizomes of the elegant bearded iris proliferate too thickly, the plants blossom less abundantly. The right time to rejuvenate the plants is after they've blossomed. To do this, use a fork to pull the bundle of rhizomes out of the soil and cut off young end pieces with one or two bunches of leaves each. Then lay the pieces of rhizomes in the bed in a circular shape, with the leaves pointing outwards. The young rhizomes are planted horizontally, with the upper third of the pieces remaining visible.

Notes / Birthdays

In this blue-purple flower bed, Turkish sage *(Phlomis russeliana)* and foxtail lily *(Eremurus)* intersperse sunny accents. Front: round-headed garlic *(Allium sphaerocephalon).* Left: Jacob's Ladder *(Polemonium yezoense* 'Purple Rain').
Garden: Bury Court (GB), design: Piet Oudolf (NL)

July

15 July

Turn your garden into a paradise for beneficial insects – by supporting them on a daily basis against all kinds of pests. With a pretty insect hotel, you can offer useful bugs a safe spot to nest and hibernate, while enhancing your garden with an attractive accessory. Place the insect home in a sunny spot close to blossoming plants. Beneficial insects and their larva need and enjoy warmth. Their domicile should ideally face south – never towards the (shady) north or the west (wind, rain) – and be placed in a raised, slightly slanted position, so that rain can run off.

Notes / Birthdays

Summer borders with unfilled blossoms full of nectar and pollen offer a feast for bees, bumble-bees, butterflies and many other beneficial insects.
Garden: Maurice Vergote (B)

July

16 July

There are two requirements for hydrangeas to turn blue: the right hydrangea and the appropriate substrate. Only pink garden and plate hydrangeas *(Hydrangea macrophylla)* can turn pure blue – red and white garden hydrangeas and other varieties cannot. In addition, this only occurs in acidic soil or substrate with a pH value below 5. Only under these conditions can the roots absorb aluminium ions, which are responsible for the blue stain. The blue turns to blue-pink at a pH value of 5.5 and above. In chalky ground, hydrangeas are therefore better kept in tubs, watered with lime-free rainwater and fertilised with "blue" hydrangea fertiliser.

Notes / Birthdays

Garden hydrangeas *(Hydrangea macrophylla)* adorn both city and rural gardens. Here, their luxuriant round blossoms frame the terrace in shades from blue to pink.
Garden: Ilka Dorn (D)

July

17 July

If your garden pond is losing lots of water, this may not be due entirely to evaporation. Particularly in natural ponds with abundant pond-edge planting, roots of marsh plants in the pond and roots of the edge planting can grow into the water. Remove these "renegades" and refill the pond. Those planning to go on a longer holiday can do so with peace of mind by pruning lushly growing plants and cleaning the filter once more before setting off.

Notes / Birthdays

Shrubs with giant leaves such as the umbrella plant *(Darmera peltata)* provide a picturesque accent near large areas of water. They can, however, seem overwhelming when located next to small ponds.
Garden: Dina Deferme (B)

July

18 July

Don't hesitate to cut flowers for vases from your blossoming favourites; by doing so, you encourage the plants to continue blooming. These tips will help your bouquet last longer:

- Cut the flowers in the morning or evening, when the buds are just showing a touch of colour or are half-open.
- Remove the lower leaves so that they don't reach the water in the vase, and shorten the stems by at least 1–3 cm.
- Add flower food to the water and stir well.
- Place the bouquet out of direct sunlight and away from fruit.
- Change the water regularly, and cut the stems again each time.

Notes / Birthdays

Framing this seat is a triad of violet, white and silver (l. to r.): biennial clary sage *(Salvia sclarea)*, Argentinian vervain *(Verbena bonariensis)*, roundheaded garlic *(Allium sphaerocephalon)*, rose campion *(Silene coronaria 'Alba')* and cudweed *(Artemisia ludoviciana)*.
Garden and design: Peter Janke (D)

July

19 July

Perennial phlox is now beginning its reign over the garden, with blossoms in white, pink, red, salmon and violet. But this is also the latest point at which any attack by stem nematodes *(Ditylenchus dipsaci)* will show itself. Thickened, shortened shoots, twisted, narrowed leaves and smaller blossoms betray the fact that the parasites have entered the plant via the leaves and leaf stalks and are rapidly multiplying inside. Chemical treatment is not possible. Remove and destroy all affected parts and place small unfilled marigolds preventatively between the shrubs. Their root excretions put the nematodes to flight.

Linking seating areas with plants through textiles creates harmony and is a proven design trick. Here, cool red and violet are the agents.
Garden: Ilka Dorn (D)

July

20 July

Lavender, the evergreen half-shrub, gives the summer a nostalgic scent and keeps aphids away from neighbouring plants. Now, in full blossom, the aroma of its violet-blue, pink or white blooms is at its strongest. It's worth cutting the flower stems and drying the flowers for scented pillows and pot-pourris. They can perfume your laundry and clothes, while also keeping moths away. Lavender sugar, on the other hand, is a treat for your palate. Crush the dried flowers in a mortar and preserve them between layers of white or brown sugar in decorative jars.

Notes / Birthdays

Olive trees in a silver-grey sea of lavender are a Mediterranean dream. Here, the fragrant half-shrub is particularly prized as a companion to roses and shrubs, and also as a structural and border plant.
Garden: private garden, Majorca (E)

July

21 July

Artistically designed gardens employ stagecraft to direct the eye along paths towards surprising highlights at their conclusions. Although these visual axes are usually defined by paths, flower beds, hedges, tree-lined avenues and arcades, this garden also integrates pools of water into its horizontal layout. In addition, it uses illusory tricks, making small areas seem larger: aisles which get narrower towards the back conjure up the impression of a longer axis and make us believe that the garden has more depth.

Even the lounge furniture is arranged to guide one's gaze in this garden. High archways of box span the visual axis like a dome and also frame the view vertically.
Garden: Daniel and Kathleen De Sy-De Smet (B)

July

22 July

Ponds and streams are used much too infrequently as a setting for roses. What a pity! For glittering expanses of water can double the plants' blossoms with their swaying reflections. However, roses should only be planted near water when the ground isn't marshy. Sleekly overhanging park and wild roses or ramblers hanging down from trees in garlands are suitable for natural ponds. Roses are not recommended for strictly formal decorative ponds and pools, as leaves and blossoms which blow into the water can quickly contaminate it.

Notes / Birthdays

This spa ensemble compactly combines a tranquil island, a pool and a water feature. The indirect lighting ensures atmospheric evenings and makes night-time bathing possible.
Design: Manuel Sauer (D)

July

23 July

Gardens can be structured not only with special elements, but also with varying surfaces and formats. A garden can, for example, be separated into different areas by using diverse surface structures, materials and colours.
The most important components for this are floor coverings, lawns, water and flower beds. Gardens whose filled and empty spaces aren't the same size appear interesting and varied. Filled spaces include planted flower beds and furnished seating areas, while empty spaces include lawns, paths, paved areas and unplanted decorative and swimming pools.

This rooftop water garden has a fascinating surface design. The static centredness of the circles contrasts with the vibrant planting, the sparkling water and the animated course of the mesh path.
Garden: Chelsea Flower Show, design: Nigel Dunnett (GB)

July

24 July

Broccoli is a treat for the eyes too. Varieties with red-violet blossoms in particular bring colour to the flower bed. When cooked, however, they turn green. This member of the cabbage family also has plenty to offer the palate. When the central cluster of flowers is not yet open, but already measures 10–20 cm across, it can be cut with a sharp knife. Afterwards, the plant should be fertilised again. This gives it the strength to continually grow small florets from the leaf axils underneath, which can then be harvested until the first frost.

Notes / Birthdays

Beans should be regularly plucked through from July onwards. The garden has transformed itself into a land of plenty, making it a joy to sit in its midst and clean and prepare the harvested crops.
Garden: Elisabeth Imig and Silke Imig-Gerold (D)

July

25 July

Many outdoor tomatoes suffer from leaf blight and brown rot. The first signs of these fungal diseases are grey-green spots on the lower leaves, which slowly turn brown and die. Later, the stems and fruit also show brown spots. Never eat affected tomatoes, as these contain poisonous mycotoxins! Unfortunately, no variety is completely resistant, but some are more or less robust. To be on the safe side, the lower leaves should be removed to begin with, and all equipment – including the tomato stakes – should be disinfected before further use. The most important precaution, however, is to protect the plants from overwatering: by installing a canopy, by ensuring a large distance between plants and by not watering the leaves.

Notes / Birthdays

The vibrant coexistence of colourful shrubs and vegetables with fruit trees and herbs around the modern beehive lends this kitchen garden its charm.
Garden: Chelsea Flower Show, design: Adam Frost (GB)

July

26 July

Design with dark foliage colours is in fashion. No wonder, since colour combinations of leaves are generally longer-lived than arrangements which include flowers. Shrubs with dark or red-brown foliage are not a species of their own but varieties of plants with green foliage. It's worth searching for them, as they make unusual combinations possible. And although dark leaves don't have much of a long-distance effect, they do become more expressive at a distance and in shade when partnered with dominant, light-coloured leaves. Plants with silver and grey foliage, shrubs with fresh green, yellow-green or white-green and yellow-green variegated leaves, as well as delicate grasses, make delightful companions.

Notes / Birthdays

Scarlet and orange-red blooms – montbretia *(Crocosmia)* 'Lucifer' and 'Firebird' – complement the brown-red and fresh green foliage. In the background: the dark leaves of white snakeroot *(Ageratina altissima)* and *Eupatorium rugosum* 'Chocolate'.
Design: Peter Janke (D)

July

27 July

Day lilies *(Hemerocallis)* are extremely popular, even though each individual bloom lasts for only one day. But more buds open constantly, often over a period of six weeks. Among the long-lived perennials there are varieties with different sizes, colours and flower shapes.
The assortment includes large and miniature blossoms, wide funnels, round flower discs, flat, star-shaped flowers, spider-like shapes, ruched and twisted blossoms, as well as simple and filled blooms and single or multicoloured flowers.
They're particularly well suited for the edges of wooded areas and ponds, in borders and close-to-nature plantings.

Notes / Birthdays

This wild perennial combination of red-hot poker *(Kniphofia* 'Tawny King'), day lily *(Hemerocallis* 'Bonanza') and goldenrod *(Solidago* 'Strahlenkrone') gleams in sunny shades of yellow and orange.

July

28 July

To maintain the lawn's velvety greenness even
in the hottest of weather, the cutting height
of the lawn mower should be raised in July.
Longer blades of grass provide the ground
with more intensive shade, helping it to endure
dry periods better. However, lawns not only
grow in height, but also sprawl horizontally.
Pay attention to exact, clear edges, which give
the garden structure.
They can be cut off regularly and tidily, or
the lawn can be kept in check by appropriate
edging (such as sunken paving stones, metal
sections or rubber edging).

Notes / Birthdays

Between fancifully pruned box hedges
and the pond, the lawn is given a quiet,
incisive structure by clear-cut edges
and a wide pool edge.
Garden: Waltham Place (GB)

July

29 July

In order for shady areas to blossom, you must not only select shrubs with appropriate light requirements, but also take into account the soil conditions. In damp, humus–rich soil, many shrubs (including beautiful, large–leaved varieties) flourish. However, the selection shrinks if the plants will be in dry soil and experience root pressure from trees. Among the favourites in this case are barrenwort *(Epimedium)*, waldsteinia, *Anemone tomentosa*, goat's beard *(Aruncus)* and white wood aster *(Aster divaricatus)*. You can also allow more light to reach the plants by trimming the trees slightly.

Notes / Birthdays

Brightening up this shady path with pink and white are shade-loving shrubs like funkia *(Hosta)*, reed canary grass *(Phalaris arundinacea* 'Mervyn Feesey'), Chinese astilbe *(Astilbe chinensis* var. *taquetii* 'Purpurlanze') and featherleaf rodgersia *(Rodgersia pinnata* 'Chocolate Wings').
Garden: Hermannshof (D)

July

30 July

Hydrangeas have the wonderful property of starting their fragrant show of blossoms in June/July, when the flowering period of most ornamental shrubs is already past, and filling semi-shaded areas of the garden with their magnificent splendour. Those who can't get enough of them can propagate them with cuttings. To do this, cut off 10-cm-long shoot tips with no buds and remove all but two pairs of the lower leaves. Dip the cutting into hormone rooting powder and plant the cutting into a pot with damp compost up to the first pair of leaves. Then place the pot in a shady spot and keep it moist. Fine roots begin to form after just two weeks.

Notes / Birthdays

After the shrubs and roses have faded in this rural atrium garden, it's time for the hydrangeas to come into their own. Fertilised weekly and watered daily, they race to bloom in pots and vats.
Garden: Ilka Dorn (D)

July

31 July

The best design trilogy for the hot months is shade, water and cool colours. Follow these rules and design a second seating area located neither close to the house nor in the baking heat, but which promises leisure hours spent under the shady canopy of a tall tree, a pergola or a pavilion, and is surrounded by secluded greenness. Furthermore, a nearby pond, pool, fountain or water feature increases the air humidity. And those who add planting in cool colour or pastel tones will also be visually refreshed, as if by magic.

Notes / Birthdays

A meeting of close-to-nature planting and formal modernity: rich in contrast yet perfect in form. The natural material wood integrates the pavilion and decking harmoniously into the green landscape.
Garden: Bury Court (GB),
design: Christopher Bradley-Hole (GB)

July

1 August

In August at the latest, you should stop giving roses, climbing shrubs, berry bushes and potted plants any fertilisers containing nitrogen – regardless of whether the nutrients are mineral-based, organic-based or mineral-organic-based. Nitrogen is the motor of all growth, but providing it to plants now would encourage the shoots' growth and make them soft. However, the supporting body of shrubs in particular should have turned sufficiently woody (lignified) and matured by the first frost, so that the shoots don't succumb to first frosts and freeze.

Notes / Birthdays

With its planting of lesser mint *(Calamintha/ Clinopodium nepeta)*, asters and black samson *(Echinacea purpurea* 'Alba'), this front garden offers a late summer feast to bees and butterflies.
Design: Ulf Nordfjell (SE)

August

2 August

Floor coverings are one of the basics of terrace design. Not only does their surface define the size of the open-air room, but their material and method of installation also shape its atmosphere. As a transition zone between inside and outside, they can link the house and the garden with their colour, style and material. Above all, however, their functional qualities should be considered. The covering must be durable, resilient, weatherproof and frost-resistant, as well as being slip-proof and skid-resistant and have a slope of 2 per cent so as to lead moisture away from the house. For south-facing terraces, it's best not to choose extremely light-coloured coverings, as they can be somewhat dazzling.

Notes / Birthdays

This terrace covers the surrounding pool like a deck. Its wooden plank flooring continues with harmoniously integrated seating arrangements and cushion chests next to the house.

Design: Manuel Sauer (D)

3 August

Floral seating enhances gardens in all seasons as an extravagant eye-catcher, giving them an aura of relaxed enjoyment. For fans of fanciful topiaries, box sofas and armchairs are perfect for expressing creativity, since the evergreen bush takes well to cutting and is suitable for baroque, playful or avant-garde designs. Those who would prefer to build something more tangible can follow the example of the chamomile bench at Sissinghurst and build a stone bench with earth in the seating area, allowing fragrant chamomile, pearlwort or grass to grow. An invitation to linger – even if it is mainly for the eyes!

Notes / Birthdays

_____

_____

_____

_____

A board as a seating surface is all you need when the rest of the body of the sofa is made of box. Amid the green organic architecture, this seat conveys a feeling of plush comfort
Design: Stijn Cornilly (B)

August

4 August

Solitary trees in a garden can be made particularly attractive by adding plants under them. Beneath old, shallow-rooting trees, this is often made more difficult by the dense tangles of roots. In this case, a mixture of earth and compost should be spread at a depth of 15–20 cm before planting – leaving about 30 cm around the trunk uncovered. Alternatively, you can plant rambling or creeping plants around the edge of the tree disc – these will cover the area over time. Examples of suitable plants include barrenwort *(Epimedium)*, periwinkle *(Vinca)*, Siberian waldsteinia *(Waldsteinia ternata)*, varieties of ivy and geraniums such as *Geranium macrorrhizum, G. endressii* and *G. himalayense.*

Notes / Birthdays

This evergreen garden is a treat for the eyes and the soul. Box shapes and an Indian bean tree *(Catalpa bignonioides)* rise above the surface designs of lawn and Siberian waldsteinia *(Waldsteinia ternata)*.
Garden: Kathleen and Daniel De Sy-De Smet (B)

August

5 August

Thyme – that delicate kitchen herb from the Mediterranean – also scores as a decorative plant. This fragrant, evergreen perennial attracts bees and butterflies and deters snails. The wide range of varieties all love sunshine and permeable, dry spots, but vary in their hardiness. Here is a list of robust varieties and types:

- *Thymus vulgaris* 'Erectus' (15–20 cm) is suitable for flower beds, edging and pots.
- Gravel beds and joints between steps and paths can be filled by the creeping *Thymus serpyllum* (5–10 cm).
- *Thymus × citriodorus* 'Creeping Lemon' and *Thymus herba-barona* (5–10 cm) have proven themselves as fragrant lawns or green roofing.
- Dry walls and hanging baskets can be embellished with *Thymus longicaulis* subsp. *odoratus* (10–15 cm).

Notes / Birthdays

Who wouldn't want to take a deep breath in this oasis for the senses! Diffusing their scent in the extensively planted beds are Mediterranean herbs such as lavender and santolina.

Design: Jan Swimberghe (B)

August

6 August

Our patience is put to the test when wasps pounce on sweet things, fruit and coffee tables. Those who have no intention of catching them with wasp traps can also try the following deterrents, which are sometimes successful:

- Hang brown paper, scrunched up into a ball, above or next to the table. It resembles a wasps' nest or hornets' nest and signals to the insects that there is already competition living here and that they should avoid the area.
- Wasps apparently find the fumes of smouldering coffee grounds and the smell of copper and brass (place copper coins in bowls on the table) unpleasant.

Notes / Birthdays

_____

_____

_____

_____

Trees on the terrace serve as an eye-catcher, a privacy screen and shade-giver. Under a sweeping canopy of leaves, not even the hottest weather is able to spoil the sociable pleasures of a summer's day.
Garden: Ilka Dorn (D)

August

7 August

In the twilight, white, silver and grey reflect more light than they absorb and begin to shine. Night-owls and plant lovers who don't get home until the evenings should put these colours close to seating areas or "illuminate" the background of the garden with them. With their white flowers, which are fragrant in the evenings, so-called night-blooming plants can be evening celebrations for the senses. Examples include common honeysuckle 'Graham Thomas' *(Lonicera periclymenum),* varieties of perennial phlox *(Phlox paniculata)* such as 'Hochgesang', 'Anne', 'Schneerausch' and 'Fujiyama', night-scented stock *(Matthiola longipetala* subsp. *longipetala),* flowering tobacco *(Nicotiana sylvestris)* and roses such as 'Blanc Double de Coubert'.

Notes / Birthdays

Even the smallest blooms of white and light pink, such as these Mexican fleabane *(Erigeron karvinskianus),* gleam in the shade. Larger flowers, of course, have a better long-distance effect.
Garden: t'Hof Overwellingen (NL)

August

8 August

Garden rooms needn't always be square. A circle brings variety to a subdivided garden. Even in long, narrow gardens, one area can be dedicated to the circle shape. With no defined direction, a circle radiates particularly centring energy and peacefulness. By way of compensation, the areas leading to the square boundaries, on the other hand, offer spaces for decorative plants, herbs and vegetable plots, or even for ponds. The circle itself can be made more striking by giving it a distinct visual accent in the centre: be it a fountain, flower bed, pond, sculpture, pavilion, sundial or an obelisk – there are many possibilities.

Notes / Birthdays

This circle presents itself as an evergreen garden room and a small water garden. The box borders, paving and decorative pool underline its shape, while the centre is watched over by a playful cherub.
Garden: Myriam Clopterop-Fleurbaey, design: Jan Swimberghe (B)

August

9 August

When salad, radishes, kohlrabi and peas have been harvested from the vegetable plot, the "second list" can be planted or sown.
- The following can still be sown for an autumn harvest: oriental greens, iceberg lettuce, endive, winter lettuce, loose leaf lettuce, lamb's lettuce, spinach, Swiss chard, bush beans, Florence fennel, beetroot, red radishes, radishes, rutabaga, May turnip, cress, parsley, rocket and chervil.
- Purchased young plants save time, allowing for the use of plants with a longer cultivation time, such as broccoli, kale or leek.

Notes / Birthdays

In a bedding square around a circle of lavender, this kitchen garden offers a variety of delicious culinary delights.
Garden and design: Peter Janke (D)

August

10 August

Geraniums and fuchsias can now be quickly propagated using terminal cuttings. Cut finger-length shoot ends from healthy plants and remove the lowest pair of leaves, along with any buds and flowers. Then plant the cuttings up to the lowest pair of leaves in compost or well-watered peat pellets, gently press on the earth, and water everything softly. As the cuttings rely on high air humidity, cover the nursery with a transparent plastic foil or hood. Place them in a bright but not sunny spot. The plants can be potted as soon as the tips of the cuttings show new growth.

Notes / Birthdays

_____

_____

_____

_____

This swimming pond can be enjoyed from all positions – whether one is sitting, lying down or part of a social gathering under the plane trees, whose crowns have been woven together to form a canopy of leaves.

Garden and design: Christian Bahl, Gärtner von Eden (D)

August

11 August

If rain fails to arrive, the garden must be watered. The best time for this is the early morning, so that damp plants can dry quickly. Alternatively, the garden can be watered in the evening – but the moisture may then attract snails and encourage fungal diseases, as the leaves dry more slowly.

Never water during the day in direct sunlight, as drops of water on leaves act like burning lenses. Above all, it's better to water generously and less often, rather than a little each day. Short-term dryness in the upper soil layers causes the roots to grow deeper, where they find more nutrients and thrive more vigorously.

Notes / Birthdays

Set above the planting and regeneration area of the swimming pond, this deck enables visitors to sun themselves surrounded by greenery. Box-shaped trees provide sculptural landmarks.
Garden and design: Christian Bahl, Gärtner von Eden (D)

August

12 August

Gardens on a slope are particularly attractive, as long as you invest in carefully considered building works to begin with. For gentle inclines, a single retaining wall is usually sufficient to create a refuge with a split-level design. Steep slopes need terracing in three or more levels, which can be designed and planted differently. The design, material and course of the retaining walls and steps characterise the garden's atmosphere. You don't need to do without the element of water. A difference in height can also be used for animated water features, water staircases or pools on multiple levels.

Notes / Birthdays

Two levels, one south-facing ensemble: here, the retaining wall accommodates features which spout water into the fountain basin below. The basin itself is connected along its entire length.
Garden: Schloss Dyck (D)

August

13 August

In order to prevent the garden from sinking into total darkness at night, lighting can be used to illuminate it and emphasise its features in the process.

Distribute the light sources into the depths of the garden and at various heights, so that the garden is perceived as a room.

- Like candles, accent lighting uses soft, unfocused light to create a selective island of light. It's suitable for illuminating paths, steps, tables, flower beds and ponds.
- Spotlights, on the other hand, emit precise, focused light. They can be installed on the ground pointing upwards, allowing plants, pergolas, archways and much more besides to dramatically emerge from the darkness.

Notes / Birthdays

Illumination has a certain magic power. While ground spotlights help sculptures and trees put on their nightly show, the animated light emanating from candles and fireplaces gives seating areas a vibrant naturalness.
Garden and design: Christian Bahl, Gärtner von Eden (D)

August

14 August

Those with miniature gardens shouldn't be afraid to subdivide them with trellises, cut hedges, archways or pergolas. Gardens which can be taken in at a glance generally appear smaller than segmented hideaways with two or three garden rooms, as these have plenty of discoveries to offer the senses. In addition, small gardens can be visually enlarged using ingenious *trompe l'œil* effects. Mirrors at garden boundaries, for example, or in partitions simulate vistas or passages, creating the impression of spatial breadth and size.

Notes / Birthdays

Dividing the narrow garden of this terraced house is a Z-shaped section of red box hedge, resulting in different garden rooms and a feeling of cosy comfort.
Garden: Birgit Thiedmann, Heinz Klink (D)

August

15 August

Roses and *Clematis* are a dream pair for archways and pergolas when they grow at the same rate. Repeat-flowering climbing roses (many ramblers grow too vigorously) and healthy varieties of *Clematis viticella,* which blooms from June to September, enter into a picturesque tête-à-tête.

- *Clematis* is planted near archways and pergolas when the rose has gained a foothold. It's planted 30–50 cm away and approximately 10 cm deeper than in the pot.
- For obelisks or pyramids, the rose is placed in the centre and the shoots led upwards along the support structure in a spiral shape. *Clematis* is placed on the outside and led to the scaffolding along supporting poles.

Notes / Birthdays

Climbing roses and *Clematis* varieties daringly put their acrobatic talent to the test on this archway. The wide box surround conceals their often bare base.
Garden: Jenny Schrijver (NL)

August

16 August

When large-flowered *Clematis* hybrids (particularly those which bloom in May/June and again in August/September) suddenly show limply drooping leaves and petals, this heralds the onset of the notorious clematis wilt. It's caused by two types of fungus which do not, however, affect subterranean parts of the plants. Cut off all shoots back to the soil – even those which have not yet been affected. The plant usually sprouts again. Those who would rather be spared such a disappointment should instead choose wild species and their varieties, perennial clematis with its increasingly diverse strains, or varieties of *Clematis viticella*. These aren't affected by clematis wilt.

Notes / Birthdays

The large-flowered *Clematis* hybrid 'Crystal Fountain' can unfortunately fall prey to clematis wilt. But who can resist the charm of its stunning filled blossoms in May/June – or its unfilled flowers in August/September?

August

17 August

The best planting time for meadow saffron and large autumn crocuses is from the end of July until mid-August. If you would like to enjoy seeing them bloom in pots, simply bed the bulbs of meadow saffron *(Colchicum autumnale)* or large autumn crocus *(Crocus speciosus)* on expanded clay, sand or gravel and keep them dry until they flower. You can also plant out these bulbs and those of other autumn crocuses – such as *Crocus banaticus, C. sativus, C. longiflorus, C. medius* – in larger groups, for example in meadows, under fruit trees, at the edges of woodland or in a rock garden. Plant them 5–10 cm deep. Because of the large leaves which appear in spring, meadow saffron needs a planting distance of 20 cm.

Notes / Birthdays

This bench proves that traditional patterns can always be reinterpreted. Protected by a roof, side walls and a back wall made of transparent acrylic glass, it embodies a modern variant of a philosopher's bench.
Design: Ulf Nordfjell (SE)

August

18 August

Sunny days and warmth help tomatoes to thrive. Now is the time to trim their main shoot, since any subsequent flower shoots will not be able to ripen before the first frost. The right place to trim is above the last well-developed flower head – above which one leaf should be left on the stem. Also remove lower leaves so that germs don't reach the foliage via spray produced when watering the plants. In addition, the suckers between the main stems and the leaves should be pinched out. Don't allow the plants to dry out, and fertilise the tomatoes weekly – especially those in tubs.

Notes / Birthdays

Free-flowering potted plants next to the house, such as hydrangeas and agapanthus, make for a friendly welcoming committee and are a charming way to link garden and architecture.
Garden: Paul Vandenberghe (B)

August

19 August

When fruit ripens, it isn't always a blessing for the tree, whose branches may break under the increasing weight of a bountiful fruit setting. It therefore makes sense to lighten the load early on. For tall trees, the heavily laden branches should be supported from below with posts and battens. Solid battens can also be used to build a tent-like structure above smaller trees before staking individual branches to these battens. For young apple and pear trees, the following year's harvest can be increased if the steeply sloped side branches are curved towards the horizontal using weights or special pegs.

Notes / Birthdays

Flickering candlelight on warm, late summer evenings transforms this bench under a quince tree into a small dream island.
Garden: Elisabeth Imig and Silke Imig-Gerold (D)

August

20 August

The secret of fragrant white lilies begins when their main representatives, the Madonna lily *(Lilium candidum)* and the king's lily *(Lilium regale),* start resembling each other. Both love sunny spots and bloom at the same time in June/July, but have significantly different planting requirements.

· The bulbs of the Madonna lily are planted just 3 cm deep in the ground and form dense rosettes of leaves until autumn. The leaves should be protected through the winter with brushwood.

· The bulbs of the sturdier and larger blossomed king's lily, on the other hand, are planted 15 cm deep in spring (in mild climates, also in autumn).

Late summer perennials popular with insects include (from l. to r.) red bistort *(Bistorta amplexicaulis* 'Firetail') black samson *(Echinacea purpurea* 'Rubinglow'), oregano *(Origanum* 'Rosenkuppel') stonecrop *(Sedum* 'Matrona') and lesser calamint *(Clinopodium nepeta).*

August

21 August

Fans of foxtail lilies *(Eremurus)* can now add these perennials with their imposing blossoms to their garden. August/September is planting time for their starfish-like root bulbs. The location should be sunny and sheltered, and the ground porous. Place the perennials, which grow up to 2.5 metres in height, in groups with at least 60 cm between them and dig out a planting hole 30 cm deep. At the bottom of the hole, shape a 15-cm-tall hill of sand or fine gravel. The root bulb, which is fragile and succeptible to moisture, is spread out flat on the hill and covered with earth to a maximum depth of 15 cm.

Notes / Birthdays

Beautiful garden images are created when structural and filling plants are used in a ratio of 1:3 – as demonstrated here by Kansas gay feather *(Liatris pycnostachya)* and black samson *(Echinacea purpurea* 'Green Edge'). *Design: Piet Oudolf (NL)*

August

22 August

There are perennial and annual types and varieties of sunflower *(Helianthus)*. In contrast to the perennials, *Helianthus annuus* has large flowers. Cottage gardens are rarely seen without them. Sunflowers always turn their leaves and flowers towards the sun, increasing their photosynthesis. This turning is made possible by one-sided longitudinal growth of the stem on the shady side. Most varieties are rich in pollen and nectar. Varieties such as 'Mezzulah', 'Double Dandy', and 'Sunrich Orange' no longer produce pollen and are therefore ideal for people who suffer from allergies and as cut flowers.

Notes / Birthdays

Yellow sunflowers *(Helianthus annuus)*, African daisy *(Osteospermum ecklonis)*, tagetes *(T. patula, T. erecta)* and zinnias *(Zinnia)* harmonise with the silver shades of snow in summer, (Euphorbia marginata), mullein *(Verbascum)*, mealy sage *(Salvia farinacea* 'Silber') and silver ragwort *(Senecio cineraria)*.
Garden: Botanical Garden, University of Düsseldorf (D)

August

23 August

Sneezeweed *(Helenium)* is a real sun-lover,
a popular treat for bees and, from a stylistic
point of view, suitable for both rural and city
gardens. It flowers extremely abundantly in
a humus-rich clay soil which is also rich in nutrients and not too dry. The prairie perennial is
especially picturesque in sunny flower beds, at
the edges of ponds, or next to a fence. Its many
varieties have single-coloured or multicoloured
blooms in yellow, orange, red and brown-red,
and range in height from 60 cm to 1.5 metres.
Early varieties begin in July, medium varieties
in August and late varieties show colour until
the end of September.

Notes / Birthdays

The sneezeweed variety *(Helenium)*
'Mien Ruys' captivates in July/August with
particularly large, brown-yellow blossoms
in great abundance.

24 August

A border's charm is characterised not only by the flowering plants, but also by structural plants with persistently attractive growth and foliage. Herbs can also perform this task. Thyme, mint (with root barrier!), oregano and lavender have earned their place in the flower bed. Leading the way are varieties of common sage *(Salvia officinalis)* with colourful foliage, such as 'Icterina' (yellow-green), 'Purpurascens' (purple-violet), 'Tricolor' (white-purple-grey green) and 'Rotmühle' (white-green). These leafy beauties tempt gardeners to indulge in both imaginative planting and fine kitchen creations, even though their sage flavour isn't as pronounced.

Notes / Birthdays

Even partners in powerful red tones are outshone by Chinese astilbe *(Astilbe chinensis* var. *taquetii),* which can grow up to 1 metre in height with intensively violet-pink panicles. A true garden favourite for flower beds and borders.

Design: Piet Oudolf (NL)

August

25 August

Set onions ripen from the end of July and sown onions from August/September. Either way, the onion harvest can begin when at least a third of the leaves are wilted and yellowed. The onions are then dug out of the ground in dry weather using a fork, and left on the bed to dry in the sun. When it's wet, they should be spread on slatted frames or in wooden cases in a shady, covered and well-ventilated place. They should be turned every two days and soil residues and loose peel removed. When the outer peel is dry, the brown leaves are woven into braids and the onions hung up – or stored without the leaves in a cool, dark and dry place.

Notes / Birthdays

Carrots, onions, beetroot, cabbage and faba beans (from front to back) thrive in this vegetable garden and guarantee a varied diet.
Garden: Elisabeth Imig and Silke Imig-Gerold (D)

August

26 August

It's wise to choose terrace furniture carefully and after trying it out, as it must meet a number of requirements. It should be:
• comfortable, which includes comfort when sitting, eating and lying down
• aesthetically pleasing and suit the house and garden in terms of size, style, material and colour
• practical and appropriate, that is to say, low-maintenance and weatherproof.
The minimum area required for seating can be calculated as follows:
Table length + 2 metres (for chairs and leeway) × table length + 2 metres (for chairs and leeway).

Notes / Birthdays

Heavy solid wood furniture needs space if it's to have the desired effect. Here, it merges with the terrace floor covering and the sunshade to create a single unit. The matching colours and materials help.
Garden and design: Stijn Cornilly (B)

August

27 August

Walls suit every style of garden and can take on a variety of functions.
- They secure the outer boundaries of your green refuge, while providing privacy and wind protection.
- Within the garden, they serve as subdivisions and also offer a degree of privacy around seating areas (with windows and delightful vistas).
- Low walls can frame flower beds, or function as seating, springheads or shelving.
- Retaining walls and terraces can take over horizontal areas from sloped gardens.

Attractive niches, seating, water features or steps can be integrated into the wall, regardless of whether its course is straight or curved.

Notes / Birthdays

This seating area can be enjoyed until late into the evening, since the dry wall of natural stone stores the warmth of the sun. It also creates space for flower beds and plants on a variety of levels – while the integrated steps provide access to it.

Garden and design: GartenLandschaft Berg (D)

August

28 August

Standard trees, obelisks with climbing plants, shaped topiary, planted hanging baskets, but also striking tall pots, garden sculptures and other accessories are twice as attractive in a pair and always a decorative eye-catcher – no matter whether they're planted out or serve as a green escort in pots to flank doors, benches, pathways and sight lines. The best results are achieved by plants with concise shapes, such as round trees, spirals or box spheres. However, it's only when the pots or climbing supports are presented in a partner look that the framework has the perfect effect.

Notes / Birthdays

Escorted on both sides by the unusual annual African fountain grass *(Pennisetum setaceum* 'Rubrum'), the gargoyle becomes a picturesque accent and is integrated into the garden's green surroundings.
Garden and design: Peter Janke (D)

August

29 August

Repeating-blooming roses are often still growing and producing shoots in autumn. This means they're less mature and more sensitive to frost than other varieties. But even frost-hardy roses can receive a new growing impulse from particularly warm and damp weather in September and October. To prevent frost damage, 40–50 g of Patentkali (Kalimagnesia) per square metre should be worked into the earth around every rose by the end of the month. It regulates the plants' metabolic processes and water supply and encourages the wood to mature, making the shoots less susceptible to frost.

Notes / Birthdays

Bring the beauty of dark-foliaged dahlias ('Bishop of Lancaster' with simple red flowers, 'Fire Mountain' with filled red flowers) to the fore by surrounding them with light-coloured flowers, silver, white- or yellow-green foliage – in this case *(Foeniculum* 'Giant Bronze').
Garden: Madelien van Hasselt (NL)

August

30 August

The original ancestor of all dahlias comes from Mexico. Its descendants inherited its hunger for sun and warmth, although they have since been bred to create so many different shapes and blooms that the multitude of varieties has been categorised into 12 types, which are still constantly being expanded. The types differentiate between single-flowered, anemone-flowered, collerette, water lily, decorative, ball, pompom, cactus, semi-cactus and fimbriated dahlias, as well as star and double orchid dahlias. An extensive catalogue of varieties with search functions for colour, height and type can be found at www.dahlie.net.

Notes / Birthdays

As if they had stored all the energy of summer, the decorative dahlia 'Valbonne' (left) and the two-colour cactus dahlia 'Jessica' (right) try to outshine each other.

August

31 August

Whether they're freshly sown or have already been harvested several times – so that chives continue to form thick, hollow stems – the magic word is "thinning". Chives will put out new shoots if you harvest from the perennial or cut them back entirely. The clumps will get larger, but the individual stems will be thinner. To avoid this, harvested clumps should be dug out every two years, the small side bulbs separated and their roots shortened with scissors. The fast alternative: simply halve or quarter the ball with a garden knife. Then plant the side bulbs or pieces of ball into a pot or bed, with some distance between them.

Secluded corners of the garden can be useful as storage for tools. Here, the clay pipes and an insect hotel also offer a habitat for many creaturess.
Garden: Birgit Thiedmann, Heinz Klink (D)

August

1 September

The lawn often suffers after the strains of summer. Drought damage shows itself as yellow patches or sparse greenery. Dethatch and loosen these areas well, so that grass seeds can germinate after sowing. The lawn can even be completely renovated, as dropping temperatures will allow grass seeds to find good germination conditions once more. Compacted and mossy areas of the lawn should be completely dethatched to allow air to reach the grass roots. Finally, the grass should be fed sieved compost or a special organic lawn fertiliser. Where moss is growing, add a little algae calcium.

Notes / Birthdays

A beautiful lawn underlines the impact of bordering areas, such as the pond and flower beds here. If you plant out crocuses or narcissi now to run riot, they will enliven the lawn in spring with bright spots of colour.
Garden: Emy and Peter Ultee,
design: In Goede Aarde (NL)

September

2 September

The optimal planting time for peonies has begun. They like deeply loosened soil without root pressure from neighbouring plants.

- For perennial peonies, the red buds on the thick roots should be covered with just 3 cm of earth. If the plants are set too deeply, they will not bloom later.
- Grafted peony bushes can be purchased in pots. For the optimal starting conditions, the grafted scion should be planted at a depth of 15 cm.
- Intersectional hybrids (a cross between the two groups) are also available in pots. They should be planted at the same depth as the top of the root ball, so that the uppermost eye is 5–6 cm deep. But more deeply located buds will also sprout.

Notes / Birthdays

Gorgeous late summer perennials: soapwort *(Saponaria officinalis* 'Plena'), perennial phlox *(Phlox paniculata)*, goldenrod *(Solidago)*, orpine *(Sedum telephium)*, bee balm *(Monarda)* and gooseneck *(Lysimachia clethroides)*.
Garden: De Tuinen van Appeltern (NL),
design: Jacqueline van der Kloet (NL)

September

3 September

With their white, pink and deep red blossoms, ornamental apples are the emblem of the month of May. The types and varieties differ not only in their blossom colours, but also in their growth, as well as in the colours and sizes of their fruit. Now their yellow, orange, red or red-brown apples make colourful, shining decorations. Larger fruit (varieties such as 'John Downie', 'Golden Hornet', 'Evereste', 'Butterball') are edible. They contain plenty of fruit acid and taste very bitter, but their high pectin content means that they're well suited to processing into jam, jelly or chutney. Smaller fruits are woody, bitter and inedible, but are charming in autumnal decorations such as garlands, wreaths or flower arrangements.

Notes / Birthdays

This roof garden has a beautiful view – not only of the river in the distance, but also of the bright red fruits of the ornamental apple 'Makamik' nearby. The trees are also eye-catching in the springtime with their purple-pink blossoms and deep red foliage.

Design: Manuel Sauer (D)

September

4 September

Autumn is a good planting time for trees. In order for a new tree to be undisturbed and grow well-rooted and vertically aligned, it needs a stake which reaches to just below its crown. This nurturing support should be sunk at least 30 cm deep into the ground directly after the planting hole is dug, in the main direction of wind. The tree is not planted until afterwards. Then, the trunk should be fixed to the stake with a coir rope or a tree tether in a figure-of-eight shape, with a crosspiece as a spacer in between. The stake shouldn't be removed for at least three years to prevent wind and weather from affecting the tree.

Notes / Birthdays

Varied lighting underlines the formal style of this modern water garden, while four ball-shaped copper beeches on the upper level define a garden room.
Design: Tuinen Brouckaert (B)

September

5 September

Hedgehogs need a safe home now, as they begin hibernating from the middle of November. The ideal spot is secluded, dry and sheltered, for example under evergreen trees or an awning. If you build up heaps of leaves, brushwood or loose woodpiles, or put up a purchased hedgehog home, you can bank on four-legged visitors. At the moment, you may also come across the cute spiny animals in the daytime. In order to survive the winter, they need to put on fat. A bowl with water, cat food with oats or special hedgehog food is perfect for them. On no account should they be fed milk, dairy products, fruit or vegetables.

Notes / Birthdays

An attractive beach chair is an eye-catcher in the garden from spring to autumn and is also a private hideaway, which offers protection from sun, rain, wind and strangers' eyes.
Garden: private garden, Majorca (E)

September

6 September

Blackberries can be grown not only along fences and trellises, but also as broad archways. To allow the archways to be walked through and harvested without painful scratches, choose a new-generation thornless variety, such as 'Loch Ness', 'Navaho', 'Loch Tay' or 'Asterina'®. These no longer taste stale and sour, but are characterised by their aroma, sweetness and frost-hardiness.

When blackberries remain partly red and even dark fruits taste sour, they have fallen victim to blackberry gall mites. Pick the affected fruits, prune the affected branches close to the ground and spray new shoots in the springtime with a compound containing rapeseed or paraffin oil when they are 10 cm in length.

A picturesque willow branch pergola animates rural hideaways and country gardens. Fresh branches sprout quickly, creating a green tunnel. On the left are the blossoms of a Jerusalem artichoke, which can also be harvested in winter on frost-free days.
Garden: private garden, Luxemburg (LUX)

September

7 September

If crisp, fresh Swiss chard with its stalks of luminous red (varieties 'Rhubarb Chard' and 'Feurio') or rainbow colours (variety 'Bright Lights') is now present in the vegetable beds, it's a real feast for the eyes. Don't hesitate to plant the splendid plants in decorative beds too! So that you can enjoy the vegetable for as long as possible, never chop a plant off completely, but instead harvest leaves from several plants from the outside inwards. If the centre or heart of the Swiss chard is allowed to remain, it sprouts new leaves. For cooking, the robust stalks are peeled from the bottom upwards.

Notes / Birthdays

This kitchen garden with its delicious diversity is green on green – but not boring at all. From the bench, you can practically see the dill, Swiss chard, cabbage, globe artichoke and onions grow.
Garden and design: Peter Janke (D)

September

8 September

Those who aren't afraid of a little hard work in the kitchen garden can harvest particularly fine vegetables. Blanching, resulting from light deficiency, hinders the production of chlorophyll, so that some vegetables become particularly tender and less bitter. Start on a dry day and blanch for three to four weeks.

• For endives, tie the heads together or place a plate over the centre of the plant.
• For celery and globe artichoke, the stalks of the plant should be wrapped up to the leaves in black film or sackcloth.
• For leek and Florence fennel, even young plants should be earthed up repeatedly. By the way – there are self-blanching varieties of some types of vegetables.

Notes / Birthdays

The autumnal bloom of larkspur *(Delphinium)* and Michaelmas daisy *(Aster novi-belgii)* frame this frugal vegetable garden, where kale, leek and Florence fennel are thriving.
Garden: Elisabeth Imig and Silke Imig-Gerold (D)

September

9 September

Between the middle of September and the beginning of October, the warmth of summer often still persists in the daytime. This stable high-pressure condition is due to continuing dry weather. It provides us with superb visibility and encourages autumnal foliage. In common parlance, such a period of good weather is referred to as an Indian summer. The gossamer threads of spider's webs we often see are mostly the work of sheet weaver spiders, which use them to sail through the air. However, the fact that so many cobwebs can be seen in the mornings is thanks to the dew, which makes the artistic weavings visible. Incidentally, the size of the spider's web tells us something about its "artist": large spiders weave large webs, and small spiders produce small webs.

This dew-spangled cobweb is reminiscent of a delicate necklace. It's the work of an orb-weaver spider *(Araneidae)*, which hangs its "flytraps" vertically. Sheet weaver spiders *(Linyphiidae)*, on the other hand, weave their webs horizontally, so that they float like fairy gossamer between blades of grass in meadows.

September

10 September

At the moment, farm gardens and cottage gardens in particular are brimming with flowers which are perfect for drying for wintertime decorations. You can simply tie the following into bundles and hang them upside down:

- Flowers from roses; lavender *(Lavandula);* globe amaranth *(Gomphrena globosa);* everlasting flower *(Xerochrysum/Helichrysum bracteatum);* pink and white everlasting *(Rhodanthe chlorocephala* subsp. *rosea,* previously: *Helipterum roseum);* statice *(Limonium sinuatum);* annual everlasting *(Xeranthemum annuum);* bells of Ireland *(Moluccella laevis);* baby's breath *(Gypsophila);* globe thistle *(Echinops);* milfoil *(Achillea)* and hydrangea *(Hydrangea)*
- Inflorescences of Chinese lantern *(Physalis alkekengi* var. *franchetii);* opium poppy *(Papaver somniferum);* honesty *(Lunaria annua)* and love-in-a-mist *(Nigella damascena).*

Flowers for drying can also be harvested from this purple-violet flower bed, for example purple amaranth *(Amaranthus cruentus* 'Velvet Curtains'), orpine *(Sedum telephium)* and paniculate hydrangea *(Hydrangea paniculata).*
Garden: Elisabeth Imig and Silke Imig-Gerold (D)

September

11 September

Those who are planting their balconies and terraces now for the wintertime need frost-proof containers. Fibreglass is thought of as a modern frost-proof material. However, this is only partially correct. Fibreglass is not one standardised material, but a colloquial term for glass-fibre reinforced plastic. It mostly consists of plastic which has been combined with glass fibres. If fibreglass containers comprise a high proportion of stone elements, these can become saturated with water, and the pots and tubs crack in freezing temperatures. Such containers are also not break-proof. When choosing fibreglass containers, it is therefore important to ensure that they are in fact winter-proof or frost-proof.

Notes / Birthdays

The iron amphorae and stoneware containers here produce a nostalgic still- life image which will become more attractive as they gain rust and patina. Since they're frost-proof, they can accompany you all the year round.
Garden and design: Peter Janke (D)

September

12 September

Stillness has returned to the garden and there's barely a bird sound to be heard. Together with other migratory birds, swallows make their way southwards between 8 and 15 September. In Germany, there's a rule of thumb which states that "The swallows leave on the Nativity of Mary (8 September)". But did you know that some species of European bat also move to winter homes in the south? While some species prepare themselves for hibernation here (they're grateful for bat boxes!), the others leave silently at night – often for southern France or the eastern Mediterranean. Like migratory birds, they probably use the earth's magnetic field for orientation.

Notes / Birthdays

The bench seat follows the curve of the dry wall invitingly. What's particularly pleasant about it now is that the natural stone stores the sun's warmth and slowly emits it once more, making it a lovely spot to enjoy the time of year.

Garden: private garden, Majorca (E)

September

13 September

"Southern living" also means treating the palate with fresh, Mediterranean delights from the garden. No wonder that chillies are becoming ever more popular. Whether they're red, yellow or green, they can be harvested at any stage. However, yellow and red varieties are the most aromatic when ripe. You can tell they've reached their optimal ripeness when they give way slightly under pressure. After harvesting, thin-skinned pepperoni can be threaded onto string and hung in the shade to dry. Thicker-skinned fruit can go mouldy when dried this way. They should be halved, dried in the oven at a low temperature and then stored in an airtight jar.

Notes / Birthdays

Roofed terraces facilitate outdoor living.
If they have a Mediterranean design, the
summer feeling lasts longer.
Garden: private garden, Majorca (E)

September

14 September

In spite of all the romance: the time when camp-fires could be lit on a whim at any time is over. In many places, a permit is required for open fires in gardens. Fire baskets and braziers are exceptions to this rule. As sources of warmth and light, they fill the longer, cooler evenings with cosy comfort.

- Braziers are shallow and made from one piece. A hole at the bottom allows water to drain.
- Fire baskets have open sides and are taller. They require a matching sheet of metal underneath, in case smouldering fuel falls out.

Many types can also be converted into barbecues with the addition of accessories.

Notes / Birthdays

Some like nostalgia, others like looking to the future. This seating area is intended for the latter, with the flickering light from the fire basket breathing life into the architectural construction.
Garden: Chelsea Flower Show, design: Andy Sturgeon (GB)

September

15 September

Romance is in and has been a trend for roses for years. It began with the English roses from grower David Austin, whose densely filled romantic flower forms and enchanting scent even bloom repeatedly during the year. They caught the zeitgeist and their huge success still encourages many growers to breed varieties and series with the charm of old roses, but which continue to distinguish themselves with their scent, their winter-hardiness and their health. Under terms such as "Nostalgic Roses", "Fairy-tale-Roses", "Painter's Roses" etc., outstanding varieties in all forms can be found now to once again cast a nostalgic spell over autumnal gardens.

Notes / Birthdays

English and nostalgic roses revive the magic of the summer in autumn. Thanks to their repeat blooming, you can bring baskets of fragrant beauty into your home once more.

September

16 September

Treasures from nature and the garden positively tempt one to create autumnal flower arrangements. The variety of squash shapes makes them perfect for this purpose too. Their branched tendrils can be trained horizontally or to climb up a trellis. To prevent the shoots on climbing supports from buckling under the weight of the fruits as they grow, they should be relieved of their burden by placing the squashes individually in nets and tying them onto the support. Fruits on the ground, on the other hand, are prone to rot. They should be protected by placing a wooden board or plate under them.

The bulbous fruits are ready for harvesting if they sound hollow when knocked on and the stems seem woody. Then they should be cut off the plant, leaving a piece of the stem attached.

Notes / Birthdays

Here, the season's flower stars (dahlia, roses and orpine) flatter crisp apples and wild fruits of elderberry *(Sambucus nigra)*, guelder rose *(Viburnum opulus)*, willow-leaved pear *(Pyrus salicifolius)* and decorative apples *(Malus)*.
Garden: Elisabeth Imig and Silke Imig-Gerold (D)

September

17 September

While gardeners often take into account the preferences of bees and butterflies when choosing plants, few think of bumble-bees. At the moment, it's rare to find one. The reason is that all the bumble-bees have already died apart from the young queens. While honey-bee workers also survive, bumble-bee communities only last for a year. Any bumble-bees now still buzzing from flower to flower are young queens searching for somewhere to spend the winter. In the springtime, each of them will be on her own: she must build a honeycomb, lay eggs and take care of the first hatching. As bumble-bees already fly out in February to begin work you can ease their tasks with early bloomers such as crocuses and winter aconite, which should be planted now.

Notes / Birthdays

The European peacock butterfly visits more than 200 nectar plants. In summer and autumn, however, it prefers red and purple flowers, such as the Italian aster (*Aster amellus* 'Forncett Florish'), which blooms from July to September.

September

18 September

Almost every farm garden contains tall, sun-loving New England asters and Michaelmas daisies.

- New England asters *(Aster novae-angliae,* approximately 50 varieties) have velvety, hairy leaves and close their flowers at night and during bad weather, even in a vase. As the lower leaves go brown and fall off during blooming (from August to September), they should be planted in the middle or the back of flower beds. They're robust and not prone to diseases.
- Michaelmas daisies *(Aster novi-belgii,* approximately 300 varieties) bloom a little later, from September to October. They need an airy spot with even ground moisture so that they don't fall victim to mildew. Only their taller growth differentiated them from bushy starwort *(Aster dumosus,* up to 50 cm).

Notes / Birthdays

The blue wood aster *(Aster cordifolius* 'Little Carlow') tolerates partial shade, but can be induced by the sun to blossom more profusely. It's ideal for natural gardens and the edge of wooded areas. This perennial blooms from August to October, and borders the shady little spot.
Garden: Elisabeth Imig and Silke Imig-Gerold (D)

September

19 September

Inexperienced gardeners often ask: "Is spring or autumn the best time to plant?" The answer is: it depends!

• Perennials which bloom in autumn (such as asters and grasses) should be planted in the springtime, as should half-shrubs and shrubs which need warmth and dryness (such as Russian sage, lavender and kniphofia), frost-sensitive summer-bloomers from bulbs and tubers (such as dahlias, gladiola and crocosmia) and frost-sensitive shrubs (such as hibiscus and hydrangeas).

• In autumn, almost all shrubs which bloom in the summertime and don't fall under the conditions above can be planted. And it's also planting time for all winter-hardy shrubs.

Notes / Birthdays

The throngs of Indian chrysanthemum (*Chrysanthemum indicum* 'Dernier Soleil') brighten this splendid double border with brilliant shades of warm yellow and apricot.
Garden: Ferdinandushof (B)

September

20 September

What would late summer and autumn be without the sun-like flowers of the coneflower *(Rudbeckia),* whose button-like dark centre continues to bloom as a little spherical head until well into the winter? Those who design with coneflowers should be aware that there are annual summer flowers and perennial varieties among the composite flowers, some of which look extremely similar. Black-eyed Susan *(Rudbeckia hirta* 'Toto Gold') is one of the best-known of the annual flowers. At just 30 cm tall, it is well suited to containers or in the foreground of a flower bed. Its rounded petals are distinctly different from the slim forms of the perennials, such as the classic *Rudbeckia fulgida* var. *fulgida* 'Goldsturm', the orange coneflower (right).

Notes / Birthdays

Between the tired red tones of orpine *(Sedum telephium,* front) and Joe Pye weed *(Eupatorium maculatum* 'Glutball', back), Deam's coneflower *(Rudbeckia fulgida* var. *deamii)* and the slightly taller Newman's coneflower *(Rudbeckia fulgida* var. *speciosa)* radiate sunny cheerfulness.
Garden: Maurice Vergote (B)

September

21 September

September is the month for harvesting apples. The fruits are ready to pick as soon as the stem can be easily twisted or snapped off the branch. The fruit should be picked using the whole hand to avoid bruises. However, not all varieties will have reached the optimal eating ripeness. Early summer apples are a juicy-sweet treat directly after harvesting, but aren't suitable for storage. Varieties which ripen later, on the other hand, require longer, variety-dependent storage periods to ripen. The best way is to store them in crates with wood shavings or paper in a cool (4–8°C), dark place. Choose healthy fruits and store them with the stem attached and not touching each other.

Notes / Birthdays

The red apples smile down from the trees as if in paradise, while below, autumn crocuses *(Colchicum autumnale* and *Colchicum autumnale* 'Album') are allowed to run wild.
Garden: private garden, Luxemburg (LUX)

September

22 September

At the moment, chestnuts aren't the only nuts tumbling from the trees. Hazelnuts *(Corylus avellana)* can be harvested when their peel turns brown. Depending on the variety, they either fall out of their shells when gently shaken or must be picked and peeled. Walnuts *(Juglans regia)* are ready for harvesting when their green peel splits and turns black. Nuts which don't fall on their own should be knocked off large trees with battens. Those which are still firmly fixed in their shells should be eaten fresh, as they aren't suitable for storage. After harvesting, the nuts are cleaned and laid out airily to dry. It's imperative to wear gloves for harvesting and cleaning, as the peel dyes the fingers a stubborn brown.

Notes / Birthdays

You could almost believe time is standing still in the golden warmth of the sun under this horse chestnut tree *(Aesculus)*. But the cool days ahead are already casting their long shadows.

Design: Piet Oudolf (NL)

September

23 September

The garden pond also needs attention this month. Remove yellowing leaves from the water, so that they don't enrich it with nutrients. Water plants and marsh plants which have grown a lot over the summer can now be removed, split and replanted. If there are deciduous trees near the pond, it's worthwhile protecting the water surface with a net before the leaves begin to fall. Mount the net above the water to prevent fallen leaves from collecting on its surface. The edges of the net should be carefully fixed to the ground so that birds don't get caught underneath.

Notes / Birthdays

Tasty treats can be found next to this idyllic pond until the springtime. Once the yellow blooms and shoots of the topinambur *(Helianthus tuberosus)* have died off in November, the delicious, healthy tubers can be harvested all winter long.
Garden: Hermannshof (D)

September

24 September

Gardeners on the lookout for something special may want to venture into the kitchen garden, where closely related gourmet vegetables from the Mediterranean are now ripe. The buds of artichokes *(Cynara scolymus)* can be harvested when the outer bracts begin to spread open but the inner ones are still tightly closed. To harvest, sever the stem approximately 10 cm under the bud.

Gourmets love the stem of globe artichokes *(Cynara cardunculus)*. After they've been blanched for three to four weeks, they should be cut a hand width from the ground and the leaves and the skin removed. They can then be cut into pieces, blanched in salt water and served with a delicate sauce.

Notes / Birthdays

White (poisonous) berries on coral red stems make the white baneberry *(Actaea alba)* an eye-catcher at the moment. It's astonishing that this easy-to-care-for shade-loving perennial isn't seen more often!

Garden: Maurice Vergote (B)

September

25 September

September is the perfect month to get the heralds of spring started. They're usually planted in groups and twice as deep as the bulb. Tulips and narcissi should be placed in the middle or back of a flower bed, so that nearby plants can later hide their unattractive wilted foliage. This can only be removed when it's brown and easy to detach. In containers, the bulbs can be planted more densely and arranged according to height. You can plant tulip and narcissus bulbs with different flowering periods in layers above one another (with a little earth in between), and even plant small early flowering plants in the soil above them.

Notes / Birthdays

Every bulb is a handful of garden bliss – at least, if it isn't soft or mouldy. The tiny power packs contain everything the plants need to germinate in the springtime.

September

26 September

The fact that autumn crocuses *(Colchicum autumnalis)* aren't often seen in gardens is probably due to the tuber plants' quirk of only forming their upright leaf rosette the following springtime. The shiny leaves of the rosette, which grow up to 25 cm long, cannot be removed until they wilt in July. This should be allowed for in the garden design and be respected. Lawn areas are mostly unsuited for the purpose. Autumn crocuses are therefore predominantly found in nature gardens, in meadow orchards under trees or near the edges of wooded areas. There, the "naked ladies" or "dames sans chemises" can expose their delicate flowers to autumn weather naked, so to speak, and without the protection of leaves.

Notes / Birthdays

Autumn crocuses *(Colchicum autumnalis)* and evergreen mondo *(Ophiopogon planiscapus 'Nigrescens')* have proven themselves to be a strong team at the edges of wooded areas – not only in autumn, but also in spring, when the large leaves of the autumn flowers appear.
Garden and design: Peter Janke (D)

September

27 September

The "queen of the autumn", the *Dahlia*, is still sometimes found in Germany under its old synonym, "Georgina". In 1791 the Spanish botanist Antonio José Cavanilles gave the floral import from Mexico the name "Dahlia" in honour of the Swedish botanist Andreas Dahl. In 1805 the same plant was mistakenly given the name *Georgia variabilis* after the St Petersburg botanist Johann Gottlieb Georgi. Although this was corrected just five years later, in 1810, the name Georgina still survives today in Scandinavia and Eastern Europe. In the plants' homeland of Mexico, they're still referred to by names given to them by the indigenous population – such as Chichipatli, Cocotli, Acocoxochitl, Acocotli and Coanenepilli.

A small taste of the diversity of more than 40,000 dahlia varieties is given by the pink-purple mottled ball dahlia 'Marbel Ball', the lilac pompom dahlia 'Franz Kafka' and the large-flowered decorative dahlia 'Vancouver'.

September

28 September

From September, evergreen plants can be planted and transplanted. This is true for rhododendrons and other evergreen shrubs, as well as for conifers. As they don't have a dormant phase, unlike summergreen deciduous plants, they'll be able to put down good roots in the still-warm ground before winter. Rhododendrons in particular require lime-free, loose, humus-rich soil. The shallow-rooted plants should under no circumstances be planted too deep, for lack of air inhibits root development and can cause the bushes to die. They aren't fertilised until the springtime. As rhododendrons like evenly moist soil, they should be watered well and mulched with leaf mould from deciduous trees or conifers.

Notes / Birthdays

Evergreen plants provide small, shady gardens with cosy permanent greenness. Here, yew cones, shaped box, laurel and cherry laurel in containers with ivy, bergenia and hydrangeas set the tone.
Garden: Bärbele and Bernhard Krug, Haus Osthoff (D)

September

29 September

Even in autumn, it's still possible to design monochrome flower beds in all colours. For example, when the focus is on pink, orpine (right) can join Chinese anemone *(Anemone hupehensis)*, asters, red bistort *(Bistorta amplexicaulis)* and dahlias in pink, boneset *(Eupatorium)*, geranium 'Sweet Heidi' and many other late bloomers.

A wide variety is also available for a "blue September": Carmichael's monk's hood *(Aconitum carmichaelii)*, blue spiraea *(Caryopteris)*, blue asters, perovskia, lily turf, hardy blue-flowered leadwort *(Ceratostigma plumbaginoides)*, geranium 'Rozanne' and fodder galega *(Galega orientalis)* help the colour of longing to make a big entrance.

Notes / Birthdays

The attractive varieties of orpine *(Sedum telephium)* liven up flower beds with nuanced pink tones and invite bees and butterflies to partake in the rich autumn menu.

Garden: Emy and Peter Ultee, design: In Goede Aarde (NL)

September

30 September

Large and small winter moths are dreaded pests. Their caterpillars move along with a characteristic arched back and eat buds, leaves and blossoms. They affect all kinds of fruit trees (except peach), but also decorative trees such as maple, oak, hornbeam, beech, lime and roses. From the beginning of October the flightless females climb up trees to mate with the males – small, grey-brown moths. Then they lay up to 300 eggs. To impede this wedding, glue rings should be fixed to the trunks now (for young trees, also to the support stake) to intercept the females. The ring must be close-fitting and lashed down under the layer of glue with wire.

Notes / Birthdays

Apples or plums which fall early often play host to the grubs of the codling moth or plum fruit moth. If they're left lying there, the larvae leave the fruit to pupate on the ground or on the trunk behind the bark. Windfall should therefore be removed daily.

Garden: Paul Vandenberghe (B)

September

1 October

Why not let the gold of October also bloom in the form of seasonal plants in tubs and other containers? On overcast days, arrangements in sunny tones conjure up some late sunshine on balcony and terrace. The autumn range includes many decorative leaf plants in these tones: gold and silver chrysanthemums *(Ajana pacifica* 'Silver'n Gold'); heather dyed yellow *(Calluna vulgaris* 'Gardengirls'); yellowish-green winter creeper *(Euonymus fortunei* 'Emerald 'n' Gold'); yellow chrysanthemums; yellowish-green ivy; creeping Jenny *(Lysimachia nummularia)*, yellowish-green common sage *(Salvia officinalis* 'Ictarine'); as well as orange–yellow and yellowish-green varieties of *Heuchera* and *Heucherella.*

This park offers a special autumn experience. As in a Gothic cathedral, the reddish-gold crowns of the common beach *(Fagus sylvatica)* bend towards each other on high trunks. In front of them are cone-shaped common lime trees *(Tilia* x *vulgaris* 'Pallida') in autumn yellow.
Garden: Schlosspark Benrath (D)

October

2 October

Facades and walls, bowers and arches show flaming red and yellow tones thanks to climbing plants. In sunny spots, these plants now say "thank you" for all the light they've received by displaying an intensive autumn colouring.

- Virginia creeper *(Parthenocissus* var. *quinquefolia)*, Boston ivy (right), crimson glory vine *(Vitis coignetiae)* and some varieties of grape vine *(Vitis vinifera)* display a luminous colour between orange and crimson.
- Trumpet creepers *(Campsis)*, bower actinidia *(Actinidia arguta)*, oriental bittersweet *(Celastrus orbiculatus)*, climbing hydrangea *(Hydrangea anomala* subsp. *petiolaris)*, common honeysuckle *(Lonicera periclymenum)*, Chinese limonnik *(Schisandra chinensis)* and grapeflower vine *(Wisteria)* all shine out in gold.

Notes / Birthdays

In autumn, Boston ivy *(Parthenocissus tricuspidata)* turns into a multicoloured miracle on sunny walls, to which it clings using its adhesive pads.
Garden: Bärbele and Bernhard Krug, Haus Osthoff (D)

October

3 October

If your enthusiasm for pumpkin makes you want to try some new varieties, you should never resort to ornamental pumpkins. Ornamental and edible pumpkins come in a variety of shapes and sizes and cannot be distinguished optically. However, ornamental pumpkins contain bitter-tasting toxic substances (cucurbitacins), which can cause serious gastrointestinal irritation and have been bred out of edible cucumbers. If you're not quite sure, try a small piece of pumpkin before you prepare and cook it. If it tastes bitter, leave it alone! Heating it up causes the bitter taste to disappear, even though the toxic substances are still present. You're on the safe side with the most popular of the edible pumpkins: Hokkaido, butternut and nutmeg pumpkins.

Notes / Birthdays

Edible pumpkins can also be combined with the fruits of physalis, Bodinier beautyberry *(Callicarpa bodinieri)* and rose-hips to create enchanting and long-lasting autumn decorations.

Garden: Elisabeth Imig and Silke Imig-Gerold (D)

October

4 October

Quinces *(Cydonia oblonga)* belong to the multi-talents in the garden, for they grace it with attractive growth (up to a height of 6 metres), large "apple blossoms" in May and brilliant yellow foliage in autumn. Most importantly of all, however, they give us apple- or pear-shaped fruits which ripen in October. Quinces are ready for harvesting as soon as they've taken on their golden yellow colour and lost their downy covering. If there's a risk of night frost, it's vital to harvest the fruits beforehand, otherwise they'll turn brown and lose a lot of their aroma. With their hard, dry pulp, they're inedible raw, but they can be used to make delicious jelly, compote or juice.

Notes / Birthdays

Quinces become more aromatic if they're left to continue ripening for a few weeks after harvesting. Pear quinces (right) are softer and easier to handle than apple quinces, but are also less aromatic.

October

5 October

Monk's hood 'Arendsii' *(Aconitum carmichaelii* 'Arendsii') enchants us once again by displaying an intense blue colour from September until the onset of frost.

However, this robust shrub, which grows to a height of 1.4 metres and is even shunned by snails, is one of the most toxic plants there are. It flourishes in sun and half-shade and loves moist, loamy soils rich in humus.

If you're looking for a lighter-coloured variant, choose the 'Cloudy' variety, which is smaller at 80–90 cm and has white blossoms with a romantic dash of purplish-blue. To curb the monk's hood's tendency to spread, or if you're working close to it, you should wear long sleeves and gloves.

Notes / Birthdays

From a distance, Monk's hood creates a similar effect in a shrub bed in front of boneset *(Eupatorium)* and asters as it does in front of golden yellow autumn leaves on the edge of the woods.

Garden: Madelien van Hasselt (NL)

October

6 October

We're well into the year, and the two herbaceous borders on the right are a real feast for
the eyes of keen gardeners – while the many
late blossoms also offer bees and other insects a
veritable banquet. Blossoming in this autumnal
ensemble (from l. to r.) are: colour-changing
oriental tobacco *(Nicotiana mutabilis),* the
simple dark-leafed dahlia 'Twyning's After
Eight', Argentinian vervain *(Verbena bonariensis),* orange-yellow autumn chrysanthemums
(Chrysanthemum indicum 'Dernier Soleil'), shrub
sunflower *(Helianthus microcephalus* 'Lemon
Queen'), red-leafed knotweed *(Persicaria /
Polygonum microcephala* 'Red Dragon'), light
purple Michaelmas daisies *(Aster novi-belgii*
'Vasterival'), and white perennial phlox *(Phlox
paniculata* 'David').

Notes / Birthdays

Yellowish-gold sun tones were included as
rhythmically repeated accents in the basic
cool tonality of these herbaceous borders.
Garden: Ferdinandushof (B)

October

7 October

Yellow clematis blossoms are missing from the range of popular large-flowered hybrids and varieties of *Clematis viticella*. However, this colour scheme is provided by varieties of *Clematis orientalis, Clematis serratifolia* and *Clematis tangutica*. These plants with their bell-shaped yellow flowers are an enchanting sight until early October. Then the cheerful sunny yellow is gradually replaced by velvety silver-coloured infructescences until the climbing plants are completely covered in fluffy tufts. They keep their downy ice-grey colour until well into late winter and then assume a glittery appearance with the hoar frost. However, the robust seed pods are also suitable for making unusual decorations indoors and on the terrace.

Notes / Birthdays

A star among the yellow-flowering clematis plants: *Clematis orientalis* 'Orange Peel', which owes its name to its succulent petals. In September/October, feathery seed tufts develop from its blossoms.

October

8 October

Wherever flower beds are more or less permanently within sight and should be easy to maintain, a good solution is to plant robust shrubs with evergreen or wintergreen foliage. In the section of a flower bed shown on the right, the combination of elephant ear *(Bergenia)* and purple spineless acaena *(Acaena inermis* 'Purpurea') plays with the threefold leaf contrast of different sizes, textures and colours. As is the case with blossoms to design herbaceous borders, here, too, it's important to plant dainty things in greater quantities over larger surfaces, whereas larg-size elements should be used sparingly. Elephant ear allows additional colour variants to be used here. For example, the 'Herbstblüte' variety blossoms a second time in September, while other varieties such as 'Rote Schwester' colour their leaves a brilliant red.

Autumn crocuses blossom late, but they do so quickly. If you plant them in late June or early August, they'll surprise you with graceful flowers in September – just like the large autumn crocus *(Crocus speciosus)* shown here.

Garden and design: Peter Janke (D)

October

9 October

When the nights get colder, especially frost-sensitive tub plants such as hibiscus *(Hibiscus rosa-sinensis)*, passion flower *(Passiflora)*, Chinese bellflower *(Abutilon)*, angel's trumpet *(Brugmansia)*, fuchsia *(Fuchsia)* and citrus plants must be put into their winter quarters. Examine the plants for pests and illnesses and carry out remedial measures if necessary. Remove withered parts and shorten excessively long shoots by a third.

By contrast, tub plants which tolerate temperatures dropping to -5°C for short periods can stay out in the open. These include oleander, olive trees, laurel trees, rosemary, aucuba, yellow sage *(Lantana camara)*, pomegranates *(Punica granatum)*, lemon verbena *(Aloysia citrodora)*, bottlebrush flower *(Callistemon citrinus)* and others.

Notes / Birthdays

Many of the annual grasses cultivated in our latitudes, such as plains bristle grass *(Setaria macrostachya* 'Will Scarlet'), also set picturesque accents in frost and snow when they spend the winter outside as tub plants.

October

10 October

In autumn, ornamental grasses are the high point of the garden. Top of the list is Japanese Silver Grass *(Miscanthus sinensis)* with its many varieties, whose foliage now turns to maize yellow, red or a brownish colour depending on the variety. Some varieties have multicoloured leaves, such as 'Zebrinus' (yellowish-green with horizontal stripes) or 'Strictus' (whitish-green with vertical stripes). From August to October, these're joined by flag-type flower panicles in silver, creamy white, rosé or brownish red which either stand upright or overhang in curves. More recent varieties are especially colourful, including 'Ferner Osten', 'Ghana' and 'Red Chief'. These shrubs are 1–2.5 metres high, become most colourful of all in full sun and look picturesque throughout the winter. Don't cut them back until spring.

Notes / Birthdays

This herbaceous border celebrates October with the reddish-gold splendour of Japanese Silver Grass *(Miscanthus sinensis* 'Ferner Osten'), red-leafed baneberry *(Cimicifuga simplex* 'James Compton'), stonecrop *(Sedum* 'Matrona') and maize-yellow tufted hair grass *(Deschampsia cespitosa* 'Bronzeschleier').
Design: Piet Oudolf (NL)

October

11 October

If you want to enrich your garden with grasses, you'll find all kinds of inspiration in other gardens and parks. Collect a few ideas and take time with your planning, as grasses aren't planted until spring. However, it's better to plant grasses which grow in clusters, for these don't use the herbaceous border as a chance to crowd out other varieties. Consider the location too, for grasses only show themselves at their best when they're in the right place. For example, golden oats (right) displays its true beauty when backlit against a dark background. It also requires an individual site and lots of space to bring out its shape.

Notes / Birthdays

The oat-type flower panicles of golden oats *(Stipa gigantea)* appear from June to August. Then the filigree yellow glumes adhere to the blades throughout the winter. Here, we see them with pampas grass.
Garden and design: Peter Janke (D)

October

12 October

The early onset of dusk can cut short your enjoyment of the garden from indoors. This can be remedied by spotlights or ground spotlights which lift trees and distinctive garden elements out of the darkness. Lighting objects become nocturnal eye-catchers in themselves and liven up the garden during the day as well. Aside from the visual effect, however, safety aspects must also be considered. This can be ensured by bollard lights, pillar lights and free-standing lights, as well as ground spikes, which can be installed next to the pathway. Alternatively, ground spotlights embedded in path and terrace coverings and garage entrances represent obstruction-free solutions. Outer wall lamps, which are also available as motion sensors, are ideal for use in house entrances and driveways and on walls and facades.

Notes / Birthdays

_____

_____

_____

_____

While outer wall lamps and ground lamps ensure safe access to the house entrance, spotlights pointing upwards dramatically illuminate the autumnal charm of the trees.
Garden: private garden, Düsseldorf (D)

October

13 October

In winter, the white bark of many birches is especially striking among trees with dark trunks. The unusual white colour of the trunks is an adaptation of the pioneers to the sun and low temperatures. For birches belong to those trees which are found at the northern-most latitudes and highest elevations. Just as whitewashed trunks protect trees from frost cracking, so the white, strongly reflecting bark substance betulin safeguards birches against overheating and cracking. The bark also contains birch tar (which makes it impermeable to water) and such a high level of essential oils that birch rind can be used to kindle a fire even in the rain. To make the white of the bark stand out more vividly, it's recommended that you wash it down now and then.

Notes / Birthdays

This garden with shrubs, trees and sculptures goes through an enchanting change of colour in autumn. On the model of Baroque bosquets, white Himalaya birches *(Betula utilis* var. *jacque-montii* 'Silver Shadow') and ribbed boxwood lozenges meet here in a geometrical formation.
Garten: Dyck Castle (D)

October

14 October

We divide up pears into juice and table variety, with the latter further classified as summer, autumn and winter pears according to their harvesting period and ripeness for consumption. All varieties can be harvested when the stalks detach easily from the branch.

- Summer pears are harvested from mid-July to September and are immediately ready for eating. A well-known variety is 'Frühe von Trevoux'.
- Autumn pears are picked from early September to November. They're then ready to eat, but can also be stored for a few weeks. 'Gute Luise' is a well-known variety.
- Winter pears are harvested at the same time. but require lengthy storage (usually from November to March) before they're ready to eat. They include the 'Vereinsdechant' variety.

Pears and pear quinces are obviously related. Whereas quinces are largely self-fertile, however, each variety of pear requires special pollination partners if it is to bear plenty of fruit.

October

15 October

Before the first frosty nights, harvest fruiting vegetables such as pumpkins, cucumbers, bell peppers and tomatoes – but also cauliflowers, kohlrabis, beans and lettuces. Tomatoes can also be harvested when they're green, after which they go on ripening indoors or on the window ledge. However, the fruits should be larger than tennis balls as their level of toxic solanine is too high otherwise. Use only relatively large fruits for making jam or chutney.

Beetroot, celery roots, carrots, parsley roots, winter radishes and autumn turnips can be stored in moist sand. For this, you need a cellar, a garden shed or a summer house with high atmospheric humidity and temperatures between 3–10°C.

Notes / Birthdays

To protect late vegetables from damage, you should get them out of the ground before the first frost. Cabbages can be kept for months in a cool place, hanging from a string (in nets or suspended by their stalks).

Garden: Manfred Lucenz and Klaus Bender (D)

October

16 October

Dahlias and gladioli have to be taken indoors before the first frost. To do this, cut their shoots back by four inches, remove the tubers using a garden fork and label them. They can then be allowed to dry upside down in a shady place. Then shake off the last traces of soil and remove empty husks and damaged parts. After this, lay the storage organs in boxes full of sawdust, straw, sand or turf, cover them up with it and let them spend the winter in a dark dry place at 5–10°C.

Dahlias in tubs can spend the winter in their tubs. Here, too, you shouldn't forget to label them after cutting them back. Put them in a cool place and moisten them slightly two to three times during the winter.

Notes / Birthdays

Dahlias are still blooming as if their life depended on it. If you really want to enjoy them for a while, remove all the blossoms, put them in a vase and prepare the tubers for their winter quarters.

Garden: Elisabeth Imig and Silke Imig-Gerold (D)

October

17 October

The further autumn progresses, the more garden waste we accumulate. Make use of the opportunity to transform it into valuable compost. Only use the remains of healthy plants and potting soil, however. If you put leaves on the compost heap, you should let them dry first. Not until then should you mix them with grass cuttings and relatively coarse chaff so that they don't stick together to form a layer impermeable to air. Rotting can be quickened by adding some algal limestone. Leaves of fruit trees, rowan trees, maple trees, hazelnut trees and lime trees rot quickly, whereas others take up to two years to do so (for example those of walnut trees, oak trees, poplars, birches, gingkos and chestnuts) and frequently contain large levels of tannic acid.

This natural garden idyll is clearly geared towards environmentally sound gardening: a wide range of domiciles offer a home to insects, whereas compost containers made of willow rods allow recycling in the garden.
Garden: Chelsea Flower Show, design: Ann Marie Powell (GB)

October

18 October

How intensely trees and shrubs are coloured depends on their genes and the climate in each case. An Indian summer is especially colourful when it follows a hot dry phase. However, it's also possible to influence the autumn colouring to a certain extent: in sunny spots with relatively dry soil and without a plentiful supply of nutrients, the leaves become more strongly coloured than they do in shady, moist places with a wide range of nutrients on offer. The colouring occurs because the chlorophyll is broken down and stored as a result of the lack of light and heat, so that the leaf colours which were covered up beforehand, such as carotine (orange) and xanthophyll (yellow) and the newly formed anthocyanins (red to pur-ple), now become visible.

Notes / Birthdays

In the case of the eastern redbud *(Cercis canadensis* 'Forest Pansy'), the leaves, which are blood-red in spring and dark red in summer, turn to yellow, orange and red in autumn. Then seed pods with a length of 7 cm appear and remain suspended on the tree throughout the winter.

October

19 October

With the help of a radiant heater, you can use the terrace until early autumn.
- Electric radiant heaters: the new halogen-quartz radiant heaters emit short waves which don't heat up the surroundings but turn to heat whenever they encounter an obstacle. They use little energy, are emission- and maintenance-free and are especially suitable for installing on walls, parasols and awnings.
- Gas-fired radiant heaters burn liquid gas from gas bottles. This allows them to be used at different locations. In the new environmentally sound models, CO_2 emissions have been largely reduced. These radiant heaters are available in the typical mushroom shape and in an attractively designed pyramid shape, and are usually made of stainless steel.

Notes / Birthdays

The trees are what give this terrace its flaming scenario: the purplish-red maple tree, the flowering dogwood in orange and the golden yellow birch in the background.
Garden: private garden, Düsseldorf (D)

October

20 October

Now, at planting time for deciduous trees, when choosing between many species and varieties, it's worth considering not just blossom, size and growth, but also autumn colouring.

- Moosewood *(Acer pensylvanicum);* golden Shirasawa maple *(Acer shirasawanum* 'Aureum'); golden Cappadocian maple *(Acer cappadocicum);* fringe tree *(Chionanthus virginicum),* Virginian witch hazel *(Hamamelis virginiana,* 'Pallida' and other varieties) and ginkgo *(Ginkgo biloba)* all shine in an exquisite yellow.
- Japanese maple *(Acer palmatum* 'Herbstfeuer' and other varieties); Mrs. Wilson's berberis *(Berberis wilsoniae);* winged spindle tree *(Euonymus alatus);* Sargent's cherry *(Prunus sargentii)* and many others light up in flaming red.

Notes / Birthdays

Japanese maple trees in yellow *(Acer palmatum* 'Filigree', left) and red *(Acer palmatum* 'Crimson Queen', right) autumn colouring provide a stylish setting for the wooden deck of this Japanese water garden.
Design: Reinhold Borsch (D)

October

21 October

If you choose the right plants, flower beds can also be arranged according to size until early October. This gravel bed owes its attractiveness to drought-tolerant, sun-loving shrubs. The softly overhanging feather grass *(Stipa / Nasella tenuissima)*, which is repeated rhythmically on the edge of the flower bed, provides for fluffy silvery tones. It contrasts with the stiffly upright column-shaped growth of the conifers and the high candles of the long-leaved bear's breech *(Acanthus hungaricus)*, which merge into decorative seed pods. A playful element is introduced by the high seed balls of ornamental onion *(Allium)*, whereas the still blooming Siberian spurge *(Euphorbia seguieriana* subsp. *niciciana)* links the partners with its airy yellowish-green.

Notes / Birthdays

The oblique rays of the run bathe this gravel garden in elegiac colours. Two Adirondack chairs, which fit in surprisingly well with all styles of garden, invite you to enjoy the last rays of the sun in comfort.
Garden and design: Peter Janke (D)

October

22 October

You should pre-cultivate the grasses in March as combinations of shrubs and annual ornamental grasses and not plant them in the flower bed until May, when they are young plants. They then stand a greater chance against competing shrubs. In many cases, you can now remove the attractive seed pods and dry them for decorative use. Just cut the stalks on a dry day and hang them upside down in an airy and shady place. The following look good and are suitable: ornamental cloud grass *(Agrostis nebulosa);* greater quaking grass *(Briza maxima),* foxtail barley *(Hordeum jubatum),* hare's tail grass *(Lagurus ovatus),* Natal grass *(Melinis repens);* African fountain grass *(Pennisetum setaceum),* feathertop *(Pennisetum villosum),* canary grass *(Phalaris canariensis);* and foxtail bristle grass *(Setaria italica, Setaria macrostachya).*

Notes / Birthdays

In the October light, the ears of foxtail barley *(Hordeum jubatum)* lie like golden veils between the slim seed pods of button snakewort *(Liatris spicata).*
Design: Piet Oudolf (NL)

October

23 October

When the season nears its end, some people want to rescue a few floral treasures quickly and keep them as souvenirs of the gardening year. This is easy to do with dried blossoms, seed pods and fruits. Just hang them up in a cool and shady place for two to four weeks. Dry, small blossoms are suitable here. Large blossoms such as lilies, which contain a lot of moisture, cannot be dried in this manner. One alternative method is to fix a wire mesh onto a wooden frame and hang the blossoms in separately, and another is to dry them in silica gel from the start. Then spray the dried plants with hairspray to preserve them.

Notes / Birthdays

What nicer way is there to say goodbye to summer than with a basket full of dried blossoms, seed pods and fruits illuminated by flickering wind lights?
Garden: Elisabeth Imig and Silke Imig-Gerold (D)

October

24 October

If you want to be able to harvest fresh chives on your window ledge at Christmas time, you should give them a rest break now. This gives the plant the impulse necessary for sprouting prematurely again.

In late October, cut back the clusters in the herbaceous border by four inches, remove the root ball and leave it out in the open in a dry shady place until late November. Don't worry if frost sets in as it does no damage to the plant. Not until then do you plant the root ball in fresh earth, water it and bring it indoors. If the plant is kept in a light cool place (at 15°C), it will go on sprouting all winter.

Notes / Birthdays

_____

_____

_____

_____

Japanese Silver Grass *(Miscanthus transmorrisonensis)* spans this herbaceous border like a peacock's fan. In front, stiffly upright clusters of switch grass *(Panicum virgatum 'Shenandoah')* stand between box spheres and feather grass *(Stipa/Nasella tenuissima)*.
Garden and design: Peter Janke (D)

October

25 October

A few shrubs also join the autumnal riot of colour displayed by the trees.

- Amsonia (including Hubricht's blue star or *Amsonia hubrichtii); bowman's root (Gillenia trifoliata);* a few species and varieties of hosta (for example the giant blue hosta *Hosta sieboldiana* 'Elegans'); several varieties of peonies *(Paeonia);* and Solomon's seal *(Polygonatum* 'Weihenstephan') turn to yellowish-orange.
- The foliage of a few varieties of elephant ear *(Bergenia* 'Oeschberg', 'Rote Schwester'), East Indian knotweed *(Bistorta affinis* 'Superbum'), hardy blue-flowered leadwort *(Ceratostigma plumbaginoides),* gooseneck *(Lysimachia clethroides)* and of a few geraniums such as *Geranium wlassovianum, Geranium × cantabrigiense* 'Berggarten', *Geranium maculatum* 'Vickie Lynn', and *Geranium sanguineum* 'Max Frei' changes from orange to red.

Notes / Birthdays

In front of the broad line of Joe Pye weed *(Eupatorium maculatum* 'Atropurpureum'), umbrella plants *(Darmera peltata)* begin to turn coppery-red, whereas eastern bluestar *(Amsonia tabernaemontana)* turns a golden yellow. Both plants like fresh, slightly moist soils.

Design: Piet Oudolf (NL)

October

26 October

There are several answers to the question as to which shrubs you should clear away in autumn and which ones you can leave where they are.

- You should cut off soft-leaved plants with little stability otherwise, like narrow-leaved plantain lilies, they'll turn to pulp in the herbaceous border. You should also cut back shrubs whose seed formation would cause them to lose too much strength and make them short-lived.
- By contrast, robust shrubs with sturdy ligneous shoots and attractive seed pods can enliven flower beds covered in hoar frost and snow. You can shorten them if you wish, but leave them as they are if you prefer them to look wintry. The same is true for evergreen shrubs.
- On no account should you prune grasses now. Wait until spring to do so.

Notes / Birthdays

_____

_____

_____

_____

Two or three frosty nights are enough to make the narrow-leaved plantain lily turn golden yellow and illuminate the shady pathway indirectly as shown here. Then they start to become soft and pulpy and should be cut off.

Garden and design: Peter Janke (D)

October

27 October

The pathway layout should match the style of the garden. In nature-like and freely designed gardens, you'll no doubt prefer curving and winding pathways in contrast to the dead straight pathways we find in formal gardens. If you cannot see the end of the pathway, gardens immediately seem larger and more interesting – even if the bend in the path leads only as far as the garden boundary. However, it's important for curves and changes of direction to be justified from the viewpoint of design. In the example on the right, it's the vegetation which prompts the change of direction. In summer, the royal fern *(Osmunda regalis)* is so large that it covers up the bend and makes the course of the pathway a surprise.

Notes / Birthdays

The pathway meanders gently through this forest garden. Before the royal fern *(Osmunda regalis)* turns brown, it fascinates us for months with the luminous yellow of its fronds.
Garden and design: Peter Janke (D)

October

28 October

In October, hedgerow roses *(Rosa rugosa* and its varieties) participate in the baroque autumnal splendour of the garden. The large plump rose-hips are then accompanied by an orange to mustard yellow leaf colour.

Many magnificent and robust shrub roses have developed out of hedgerow roses. These are characterised by the wrinkly foliage and the bushy growth of the shoots, which are densely covered in prickles and bristles. It's no wonder that many *Rugosa* derivatives prove their worth as impenetrable hedges and ground covers. Many of them continue producing a profusion of new blossoms while the rose-hips develop their colour.

Notes / Birthdays

This rose hedge has a rich harvest of rose-hips to offer. All types of rose-hips are suitable for making jams and purees, but the most productive of all are of course the large-fruit varieties.
Garden: Madelien van Hasselt (NL)

October

29 October

Fountain grasses *(Pennisetum)* have their finest hour at this time, for this is when their leaves and blades turn to luminous maize yellow, whereas the fluffy inflorescences take on silvery-white or reddish tones. The most popular perennial representatives include *Pennisetum alopecuroides* with its numerous varieties and *Pennisetum orientale.* Just like their annual relatives (such as *P. setaceum, P. villosum),* they form attractive clusters with no runners. If you're disappointed with perennial fountain grasses because they won't blossom, you should note down (in your diary for example) which plants are involved. You'll have to rejuvenate them by dividing them up in spring as this will stimulate them to flower again.

Notes / Birthdays

The repetition of distinctive plants gives the garden structure and rhythm. Here, the classic woolly white fountain grass *Pennisetum alopecuroides* 'Hameln' accompanies the staccato of the cypresses.
Garden and design: Peter Janke (D)

October

30 October

It's high time to autumn-clean the pond. Remove leaves and plant remains thoroughly using a scoop and drain off three quarters of the water in the case of small and medium-size ponds. This makes it easier to catch the fish and put them into a substitute pool. Then remove the decaying organic matter from the bottom and brush the algae from the walls of the pond film. You can also use the opportunity to cut back strongly all proliferating plants. Do not, however, lop off cane brake and reeds, but tie them together instead. Then fill up with fresh water and put the fish back in. In relatively large ponds, this annual cleaning isn't necessary, but leaves and proliferating plants should at least be removed.

Notes / Birthdays

As soon as the water temperature drops below 10°C, many fish stop feeding and fall into a kind of hibernation and should therefore no longer be fed.

Garden: Madelien van Hasselt (NL)

October

31 October

The grasses come into their own when the blossoms gradually begin to take their leave. Many perennial grasses have developed into distinctive autumnal beauties, whose colouring or flower panicles attract our gaze. Make sure you keep these delightful structures, as they'll adorn the garden throughout the entire winter. Some of the most remarkable ones are reed grass *(Calamagrostis* with species and varieties), Japanese Silver Grass *(Miscanthus sinensis* with many varieties), moor-grass *(Molinia* with species and varieties), switch grass *(Panicum virgatum* with varieties), Chinese fountain grass *(Pennisetum alopecuroides* with varieties), Indian grass *(Sorghastrum nutans)* and pampas grass *(Cortaderia selloana* with varieties).

Notes / Birthdays

Reaching the peak of its beauty amid this festival of impermanence is Korean feather reed grass *(Calamagrostis brachytricha)*. In the foreground of the herbaceous border, we can see withered *Echinacea* and the foliage of the astilbes, which have turned brown.

Design: Piet Oudolf (NL)

October

1 November

The frost gives a metallic shine to the leaves of the Chilean rhubarb *(Gunnera manicata),* which can reach a diameter of up to 2 metres. The first frosts make it turn dark and limp. Below –8°C, however, a lack of winter protection can be life-threatening for this shrub with its decorative leaves. This is why you should now cut off its leaves and shorten the stalks to a length of 30 cm. In mild regions, you can protect the plump rhizomes by covering them with overlapping leaves positioned upside down (see 3 December). In cold regions, we recommend putting a large wire cage over the plant and filling it with a mixture of tree cuttings, leaves, brushwood and coconut fleece. To prevent moisture from penetrating and leading to rot, lay boards or a film on the top.

Notes / Birthdays

_____

_____

_____

_____

Here, a few young giants gather round the bald cypress *(Taxodium distichum).* This mammoth-leaved plant is accompanied by giant miscanthus *(Miscanthus* x *giganteus),* Himalayan knotweed *(Aconogonon polystachyum)* and Japanese Silver Grass *(Miscanthus sinensis* 'Flamingo').
Garden and design: Peter Janke (D)

November

2 November

Tree and shrub protection involves many different aspects. Evergreen trees and shrubs such as box, holly, rhododendrons and conifers should now be watered more frequently and more intensively, especially after a dry autumn and in soils containing little water. This is because moisture evaporates through their leaves, even in winter, without their being able to draw fresh moisture from the frozen ground. You should also water them as soon as the ground has thawed after relatively long periods of frost. In the case of freshly planted young trees and shrubs, protect the root area using a layer of mulch consisting of chaff and leaves. In regions with permanent and long late frosts, use fleeces to give young evergreens in sunny spots extra shade.

Notes / Birthdays

After frosty nights, deciduous trees no longer display their brilliant show of colour, and evergreens such as the cypresses shown here *(Cupressus sempervirens* 'Atropurpurea') then become the dominant features in the garden.
Garden and design: Peter Janke (D)

November

3 November

The sensitivity to frost of trees and shrubs (and roses too) depends on a number of factors:
• The genus, species and variety of plant
• The age of the plant. Younger examples are always more sensitive to frost than older ones which have already adapted to the climate.
• The weather. Plants can withstand low sub-zero temperatures better when they fall gradually than when they drop abruptly.
• The fertiliser used. Giving trees and shrubs fertiliser containing nitrogen from July onwards stimulates their growth. Their shoots remain soft and succulent, so that they don't become sufficiently ligneous by the time frost sets in. This is why you should stop using full fertilisers from late July onwards as they all contain nitrogen.

Notes / Birthdays

Like small flames, the seed pods of Korean mint *(Agastache rugosa)* dance in front of the smokewood *(Cotinus dummeri* 'Grace'), whose dark purple foliage bids farewell with a fiery scarlet.
Garden and design: Peter Janke (D)

November

4 November

In cold regions, fish, amphibians and winter-hardy aquatic plants can only spend the winter in ponds which have a depth of at least 1.2 metres over a relatively large area because these parts don't freeze. The easiest way to get water lilies and other aquatic plants through the winter safely is to put them into planting baskets. Cut them back and place the baskets in the deepest part of the pond. Winter-hardy shallow-water varieties are simply put back in shallower places in spring. In the case of ornamental pools with vertical walls, the water must be removed. Here, as in shallow ponds, place the water lily baskets in a water-filled trough and allow them to spend the winter indoors in daylight at 10°C like exotic aquatic plants.

Notes / Birthdays

"Kettledrum and harp" is the name which Karl Foerster gave to the distinctive contrast between large round leaf shapes and linear ones. Here, we can see water lily leaves combined with reeds silvery from the frost.

November

5 November

Large and impressive shrubs such as the highly toxic aconite *(Aconitum)* often have shoots with hollow stalks which nevertheless remain stable throughout the winter. Leave them in the herbaceous border and don't cut them back until spring. However, if you want to tidy up the flower bed by transplanting, redesigning, rejuvenating or subdividing the plants, and if you live in a region with a lot of rainfall, you should shorten these hollow-stalked shrubs to a length of 15-20 cm on a dry day instead of cutting them back to the width of your hand. Then snap off the short shoots. As a result, neither rain nor dew can collect in the stalks and lead to rot. Don't cut them back radically until spring. Important note: always wear gloves when handling aconite!

Notes / Birthdays

The robust blossoms of Carmichael's monk's hood *(Aconitum carmichaelii)* and bluebeard *(Caryopteris* x *clandonensis)* withstand the frost for a time and retain their colouring before they expire in powdery beauty.

November

6 November

The crystalline beauty which the frost gives to Japanese anemones can only be enjoyed for a short period now, and should then be cut back. These normally easy-to-maintain shrubs require some winter aid during the first few years. This is the reason why you should cover them with brushwood after pruning them back. Japanese anemones are always grateful for this treatment in cold regions and when there is black frost. If you fall in love with the elegant dance of their graceful blossoms in late summer, however, you should on no account plant them now as they must be planted in spring. Until then, take your time choosing from the distinctive varieties and think carefully about where to locate them, because it's difficult to get rid of these spreading beauties once they've settled.

Notes / Birthdays

The pink petals of the beautiful new Japanese anemone (*Anemone hupehensis* 'Rosenschale') are darker-coloured at the edges and back. Now hoar frost and frost have made its last blossoms go pale.

November

7 November

When water makes the transition from the liquid to the frozen state, its volume increases by almost 10 per cent. We speak of the anomaly of water in this case, as the volume of all other liquids becomes smaller when they're cooled down and frozen. If there is still water in pipes, hoses, pumps, barrels, pools and containers with high vertical walls, the ice cannot expand upwards, so it will break through the walls. This is why you should empty water hoses, pools and all containers with vertical sides in good time before the first frost. Then cover them up, give them shelter or take them indoors so that snow, rain and dew cannot accumulate in them during winter.

Notes / Birthdays

The time of romantic water music coming from fountains and gargoyles is over. As a precaution empty fountain and water connections and close the supply pipes.
Garden: Kristin Lammerting (D)

November

8 November

Even in the inhospitable month of November, the garden still produces fresh green for the table: like lamb's lettuce *(Valerianella locusta),* spring beauty *(Claytonia perfoliata)* is sown and cultivated from September onwards. You can put it on the table as a salad or steamed. The leaves sprout again when the heart stands still. Neither permanent frost nor snow can harm spring beauty and lamb's lettuce provided you cover them up with fleece or brushwood over-night. However, the protective cover should be removed again during the day as lamb's lettuce in particular would otherwise store more nitrates. The longer it's left in the herbaceous border, the more nitrates it accumulates. This is why you should harvest it in good time and in the evening because the nitrate level is then lower.

Notes / Birthdays

Chard is usually grown only annually. However, if you cut off the leaves and cover up the roots with brushwood, straw or leaves, you can harvest fresh shoots again in spring. Chard doesn't become inedible until it starts to run to seed.

November

9 November

Cabbage – the traditional winter vegetable –
has long lost its dull image and acquired gourmet status. The typical round cabbage varieties
white cabbage, red cabbage and savoy cabbage
can only withstand below-zero temperatures
for a very short period. This is why they
should be harvested before the frost sets in and
stored in a moist, cool and dark place. Red
and white cabbage actually keep for months
if you wrap packing tape round the stalk and
then hang them upside down from a taut rope.
Green cabbage and Brussels sprouts can stay
in the bed longer, since cold helps them to
develop their full aroma. They store sugar after
slight frost (down to –10°C) or if they've at
least been in the bed at low temperatures.

Notes / Birthdays

In contrast to pumpkin, savoy cabbage –
like white cabbage and red cabbage – can
withstand temperatures down to -5°C for short
periods. If it is not protected by fleece or film
at below-zero temperatures in the herbaceous
border, it should be harvested by November.

November

10 November

For almost five months, greenhouses will now become the main focus of life for keen gardeners. To make sure they're worth using during the winter, you should clean the panes now and insulate your little crystal palace with bubble wrap.

Even a winter temperature of just 2–12°C offers a multitude of uses. A cold store of this kind is a suitable domicile for many tub plants, a depot for frost-sensitive onions and bulbs (such as dahlias, gladioli and canna) and storable vegetables and a place in which to keep gardening utensils and fertiliser.

However, special collections of plants (such as cacti, camellias and bonsais) can spend the winter under optimum conditions there too. Last but not least, you can also cultivate winter-hardy lettuce, spinach, lamb's lettuce, chives and chicory in the greenhouse.

Cavolo nero 'Nero di Toscana' (also known as Tuscan cabbage or black cabbage) is a Tuscan green cabbage that can withstand temperatures down to -5°C, and even slightly lower, when protected under fleece. When you harvest it, you should only pick four to five leaves per plant from bottom to top.

Garden and design: Son Muda Gardens, Majorca (E)

November

11 November

To ensure that floribunda roses, hybrid tea roses and shrub roses get through the winter well, remove all leaves from the shoots and the ground, for fungal illnesses can survive the winter in them. Then cut excessively long shoots back slightly and shovel soil around the foot of the roses to a height of 20–30 cm. In the case of weeping standard roses, which have been bred to a stem height of up to 1.4 metres, pull the branches of varieties with soft shoots downwards and tie them to the stem. In the case of squarrose varieties, shorten the shoots by a third and then protect the bud union with a material pervious to air, such as spruce brushwood, wood wool, polystyrene wool or straw. Then put a jute sack, a special fleece or a rose cover over them and tie it at the bottom.

Notes / Birthdays

In order not to pamper the roses, it's sufficient to wait until late November before providing winter protection. Never use plastic bags, as the condensate which forms in them can freeze and cause damage.

November

12 November

When deciduous trees display their autumnal colours and draw valuable nutrients from their leaves and store them, another process starts at the same time: a thin layer of cork forms between the twigs and the leaf stalks. This separating tissue closes the nodalities and prevents parasites and germs from penetrating into trees or shrubs. Once the layer has turned to cork, a puff of wind is enough to release the leaf. By shedding their leaves, trees and shrubs get rid of huge evaporation surfaces which would otherwise cause them to dry out if they were unable to draw any more water from the frozen soil. For example, a horse chestnut sheds an average of up to 25 kg in leaves, and a birch as much as 28 kg.

Notes / Birthdays

The bioclimatic architecture of beech arch and beech hedge enlivens the garden with its warm brown tones until new shoots appear. The reason is that the dry leaves often stay on beeches and oaks until spring and give hedges a certain degree of opacity in winter.
Garden: De Wiersse (NL)

November

13 November

When the garden goes into hibernation, it's time to tend to the gardening equipment. To ensure that you can continue to enjoy the benefits of gardening implements for as long as possible, you should clean them thoroughly before putting them into storage. Remove soil and decayed matter from metal tools such as lawnmowers, spades, forks and shears using a coarse brush and remove rust using a wire brush or sandpaper. Then sharpen the lawnmower knives, blades and the edges of spades and rub non-resinous machine oil onto them. Also, don't forget to sand down rough wooden handles and apply linseed oil to them.

Notes / Birthdays

A greenhouse is an ideal depot for pots and tubs you don't need just now. The containers must be cleaned first, however. You can remove calcium deposits by putting them into vinegar or potato water and then scrubbing them down with a brush.

November

14 November

It's becoming increasingly popular to fill containers and tubs with seasonal plants. If the combinations are to display fresh colour until spring and not fall victim to frost, it's important to choose the right plants.

- Instead of *Erica gracilis,* which is now being offered en masse, use the bud-blooming heather *Calluna vulgaris* Garden Girls, which is available in many different colours. *Erica gracilis* soon sheds its blossoms, whereas *Calluna vulgaris* retains its colourful buds.
- Don't use silver ragwort *(Senecio cineraria)* – use the silvery-white cushion bush *(Leucophyta brownii)* instead. Ragwort turns brown after the first night frosts, while cushion bush keeps its shape and colour all winter long.

Notes / Birthdays

Heather in yellow, pink and white, pink and white prickly heath *(Gaultheria/Pernettya mucronata),* red snowberry *(Gaultheria procumbens),* silverleaf, dwarf conifers and wintergreen shrubs and cones make a garden attractive throughout all periods of frost.
Garden and design: Peter Janke (D)

November

15 November

Heat-loving evergreen pampas grass *(Cortaderia selloana)* needs protection against heat and moisture. Tie its 1.8–2.5-metre-high shoots together like a tuft so that rain and snow cannot penetrate into the cluster. Then heap dry leaves around the plant and weigh it down with brushwood or wire mesh. It's vital to wear gloves to protect your hands from the razor-sharp edges of the blades of grass! Low varieties only reaching a height of 1–1.2 metres such as 'Pumila' or 'Evita' are suitable for putting in tubs too. They're also tied together and, like other tub plants, can stay outside for the winter (see 26 November) or be kept in a light, cool and frost-free spot in a garden shed or greenhouse. Don't forget to water them!

Notes / Birthdays

You usually plant the stately pampas grass *(Cortaderia selloana)* and the elegant golden oats *(Stipa gigantea)* as solitary plants in herbaceous borders. Here, they prove that they can also become eye-catchers as part of a team effort.

Garden and design: Peter Janke (D)

November

16 November

It's almost a bit too late in the year to sing the praises of red bistort *(Bistorta amplexicaulis,* also available commercially as *Persicaria amplexicaulis* and *Polygonum amplexicaule)* and its beautiful varieties. However, these robust and long-lasting stars of late summer are worth keeping in mind for the next season. They blossom from July to October and form compact clusters in sun and half shade. Their white, pink or red flower spikes appear above them. The 'Spotted Eastfield' variety also has white speckled foliage.
To cap it all, these shrubs are shunned by snails and can even withstand the root pressure of trees. This allows them to be used in a variety of ways, be it in flower beds or herbaceous borders or at the edge of a pond or clump of trees.

Notes / Birthdays

The 'September Spires' and 'Rowden Gem' varieties expand the range of red bistort *(Bistorta amplexicaulis)* with purplish-pink and flower until early November.

November

17 November

If you want to make ornamental grasses fit for the winter, be aware that neither summer grasses nor evergreen grasses should be planted or cut back now.

- With summergreen grasses, the upper third of moisture-sensitive species and varieties such as pampas grass (see 15 November), Japanese Silver Grass *(Miscanthus sinensis)*, Spanish cane *(Arundo donax)*, Indian grass *(Sorghastrum nutans)* and pennisetum *(Pennisetum)* are tied together like a tuft. This stabilises them even when snow falls. You should also protect them at the base by sticking spruce twigs into the soil at an angle or piling leaves around them.
- Evergreen grasses need no protection. Don't cut them back in spring but just clean them up instead.

Notes / Birthdays

In regions with mild winters and little rain, grasses can display their encounter with hoar frost all through the winter. In this circular flower bed, *Poa labillardieri* grows below silver willows and is flanked by *Miscanthus* x *giganteus* (back) and *Miscanthus sinensis* 'Silberfeder' (right).
Garden and design: Peter Janke (D)

November

18 November

Climbing and rambler roses are found on free-standing trellises such as rose arches, obelisks, columns and pergolas, often in exposed locations with little shelter. Winter protection is a three-point programme here:

- Remove all the leaves from the plants and the ground so that spores of fungal diseases cannot hibernate in them.
- Pile up soil around the base to a height of 20–30 cm.
- Protect the shoots from wind, sun and frost. To do so, loosely wrap sacking, jute or bamboo mats or reed or straw mats around them. Alternatively, you can insert spruce brushwood overlapping from bottom to top like roof tiles so that rain and dew can run down the outside of the rose.

Notes / Birthdays

_____

_____

_____

_____

In contrast to climbing roses, grapevines *(Vitis vinifera)* don't require any winter protection. Here, a red-leafed Japanese maple leans against its trunk as if needing support.

November

19 November

A bird the size of a tit loses 2 grams of weight in one winter night – which is about 10 per cent of its body weight. To survive this, it has to find plenty of nourishing food the next day. It helps if as many seed pods of grasses, shrubs and wind fruits as possible have been left standing. In most cases, however, this won't be enough, which is why you should wait no longer before starting to feed the birds. Offer soft feed and grain feed at several places which the birds can see right into and which are safe from cats. Attractive bird houses and hanging feeders enrich the garden with beautiful accents and soon attract a lively collection of birds that is wonderful to watch from your window.

Notes / Birthdays

What floral magnificence shrubs (*Sedum* and *Lavandula* in this case) and grasses now present when hoar frost gives contour to their growth! The seed pods of many of them provide birds with a few last crumbs and help them to make the transition to the severity of winter.

November

20 November

Few plants can rival the exoticism of red-hot pokers *(Kniphofia),* whose tall inflorescences appear from July to September. This is no surprise, for these evergreen shrubs with their grass-type clusters come from southern Africa and the Arabian Peninsula. Full sun, permeable chalky soil and a sheltered winter domicile are basic requirements for them to thrive in our latitudes. Now you should twist the grass-type leaves together, tie them up tightly and cover everything with brushwood. This protects the heart of the plants from cold, moisture and winter sun. *Kniphofia caulescens* 'Short Garden Form' and varieties such as 'Alcazar', 'Royal Standard' and 'Safranvogel' are extremely winter-hardy.

Notes / Birthdays

Grasses such as *Calamagrostis brachytricha, Calamagrostis* x *acutiflora* 'Karl Foerster', *Chasmantium latifolium, Molinia caerulea* 'Transparent' and shrubs such as *Sedum* 'Matrona' and *Kniphofia caulenscens* 'Short Garden Form' remain all winter long.
Garden and design: Peter Janke (D)

November

21 November

A lean-to greenhouse will give you twice as much enjoyment if it's comfortably furnished. If the temperatures in it don't drop below zero, it's an ideal winter domicile for citrus plants and other tub plants which are hungry for light. However, before the sowing and pre-cultivation of summer flowers and vegetables begins in early spring, it becomes the gardener's treasure trove in which to store gardening implements and seeds, but also fertiliser and pesticides, which have to be protected from the frost too. In addition, you can use it as a place in which to pore over new plant catalogues, complete your garden diary and make and sketch new plans for the garden.

Notes / Birthdays

Sitting in this "crystal palace" is like being in a vine bower. Even in the cold season, it allows the gardener to enjoy at close quarters some beautiful things which are better kept in a protected place over the winter.

Garden: Josje Reuten (NL)

November

22 November

Heated conservatories offer a wealth of advantages because this comfortable light-filled environment is like an open-air living room. If you use the blessings of modern technology, you can reduce the effort and maintenance required and increase the level of comfort. Self-cleaning glass is extremely practical: thanks to its special coating, the rain washes off all dirt particles. Intelligent technology even lets you control many things centrally without having to press buttons all the time. For example, an indoor sensor can regulate room temperature and moisture by activating blinds, awnings, heating and ventilation.

Notes / Birthdays

You can live like a prince in this glass house with its crystal chandelier and its aviary while being very close to the world of the garden outside.

Garden: Hoof's Hoof (B)

November

23 November

When the garden goes into hibernation, your love of plants can concentrate on putting the garden waste to good use and creatively decorating your home:

- Seed pods, dried blossoms, late fruits and bizarrely shaped branches can be transformed into unusual decorations.
- Home-made chutney made of fruits from the garden makes a wonderful present.
- Home-blended tea made of blackberry, raspberry and strawberry leaves and finely flavoured with rose hips, mint, lemon balm, lavender, hibiscus and whatever else the garden provides will bring back memories of summer. Dry everything well, crumble it up and then keep it in a cool dark place.

Notes / Birthdays

Here, holiday souvenirs such as seashells and snail shells have been arranged with foxtail lily blossoms and ivy vines to form an elegant ensemble.
Garden: Lidy van Sorgen (NL)

November

24 November

Make the cleared vegetable beds fit for the winter by loosening up the soil and weeding again before the frost sets in. In the case of heavy loamy soils and weed infestation, turn the soil over in coarse clods. This mixes up the soil layers, but it also aerates the ground and enriches it with plant remains and weeds. Over the winter, the frost loosens the coarse clods, leaving a crumbly structure behind in spring. In the case of soil rich in humus, it's sufficient to loosen it with a single-prong sowing hoe. Mix in semi-mature compost, stone dust and algal limestone. Then mulch the surface of the herbaceous border with straw, grass or grass cuttings. Finally, cover everything up with brushwood or a net so that the wind doesn't blow away the mulching material.

Notes / Birthdays

The flowers, herbs and vegetables in the four segments of this herbaceous border surrounding a small circular bed will soon fall victim to frost. This means it is worthwhile harvesting a few final treasures while there's still time.
Garden and design: Peter Janke (D)

November

25 November

Not all ferns give hoar frost the opportunity to create patterns like the wintergreen Japanese shield fern. The fronds of summergreen ferns don't offer this spectacle as they're now turning brown. However, they don't need much winter protection as their rhizomes are protected by the fronds above them. By contrast, wintergreen ferns require a spot in which they're protected from the winter sun, or they should be covered with brushwood or fleece if necessary.

There are species and varieties of summergreen and wintergreen ferns which grow in clusters or sprout runners. For small shady surfaces and combined flower beds, it's important to choose a fern which grows in clusters.

Notes / Birthdays

Here, hoar frost reveals the picturesque regularity of the double-pinnate fronds of the wintergreen Japanese shield fern *(Dryopteris erythrosora)*. In spring, its foliage is joined by a bronze-coloured shoot with orange-red fronds which later turn to a fresh green.

November

26 November

Trees and shrubs which spend the winter outside in tubs require threefold protection.
- Put every tub next to the house in a spot sheltered from the wind and place it on a polystyrene base, which functions as a buffer against the frost. Put wooden blocks and the tub onto it in such a way that the water drainage holes aren't blocked.
- Wrap bubble film, sacking or coconut mats around each pot. In extremely cold regions, you can fill up the gaps with insulating material such as polystyrene chips or leaves.
- Protect sensitive above-ground parts of the plant using fleeces, sacking or brushwood and cover the top of the root ball with coconut chips, wood wool or brushwood.

Notes / Birthdays

The frosted blossoms of the willow-leaved loosestrife *(Lysimachia ephemerum)* look as if made of sugar. This shrub tolerates temperatures down to -10°C. In very cold regions, it should winter in or next to the house. It's seen here in front of the red autumn foliage of sacred bamboo *(Nandina domestica)*.

November

27 November

From November onwards, the garden starts to looks different. With the beginning of hibernation, the vigorous colours of autumn are replaced by the subtle white and silver tones of fog and hoar frost. When herbaceous growth has stopped, gardens often look empty. How nice, then, when sturdy shrubs and grasses or evergreen and wintergreen trees and shrubs take over! Their shapes and subtle colours fill gardens with lines, surfaces and accents to which the hoar frost gives additional plasticity. Wherever elements with stable structures are lacking, you should write notes or take photographs and use the winter to plan improvements.

Notes / Birthdays

The contrast between emptiness and abundance makes gardens dynamic in winter too. Here, two column-shaped thuja look like exquisite sculptures gracing the calm lawn.
Garden and design: Peter Janke (D)

November

28 November

For a garden to be perceived as a self-contained space, it requires a permanent structure which defines it and gives the observer protection and shelter. The basic conditions change once the accompanying plants have gone. Then we perceive hedges, fences and walls as distinct entities. This shows how valuable it is to select plants and materials carefully and arrange them to subtle effect. Original windows, openings or imaginative silhouettes transform cut hedges into striking boundaries.

Fences can underline the style of the garden with a strictly formal or a wildly romantic country look, while walls can liven up the austerity of winter with attractive trellises or bright colours.

Notes / Birthdays

It's worthwhile arranging garden elements in an attractive way. Features which are obscured by clematis and rose blossoms and overgrown with shrubs and grasses in summer now come to light – like this beautiful wrought-iron fence.

Garden and design: Peter Janke (D)

November

29 November

"Driftwood" is an occasional alternative name for recycled teak (also known as old teak), which is currently a popular trend in garden furniture. A large part of this wood comes from demolished houses, disused benches and ships in Indonesia. Recycling the wood makes it unnecessary to fell trees. It's cleaned, sanded and brushed carefully before being used to make new furniture. In some cases, care is taken to preserve marks of use or traces of paint. Although teak is frost-free, this furniture should be kept in a dry and sheltered place for the winter if there is no explicit indication that all other materials used are able to withstand our winters.

Notes / Birthdays

Just like these old wooden implements and pieces of driftwood, stones, roots and found wood overgrown with moss and lichen can also bring nature directly before your eyes in the form of winter-hardy decorations.

Garden: private garden, Majorca (E)

November

30 November

The European larch *(Larix decidua)* belongs to the pine family *(Pinaceae),* but it's the only domestic conifer whose needles turn to gold in autumn before the tree sheds them. Its airy cone-shaped growth, its golden needles in autumn and its pastel green shoots in April make it a very elegant, bright and friendly tree (height: 35 metres) for large or park-like gardens. To ensure that its branches stay on the tree right down to the bottom, larches should be planted in a sunny spot as a solitary tree if possible. They can withstand temperatures down to –35°C without difficulty; they and yews have the hardest wood of all domestic conifers.

Notes / Birthdays

Covered in hoar frost, the needles of the Japanese larch *(Larix kaempferi* 'Diana') are reminiscent of starflowers. This slowly growing tree only reaches a height of 8 metres. With its bizarre and airy growth, it also fits well into smaller gardens as an attractive solitary tree.

Garden and design: Peter Janke (D)

November

1 December

Trellises and structural elements which serve as an aid for climbing plants shouldn't be just functional – they should be attractive too. To regard trellises as second-best after the plants would be to overlook many creative visual oppostunities, for in the low-foliage half of the year, that is to say, from November to April, they clearly take centre stage.

The material, shape and colour of pavilions, pergolas, obelisks, climbing walls and trellises shouldn't only match the form and style of the garden but also make it more attractive. Even if these elements are obscured by foliage and blossoms for half of the year, they become a decorative element in the garden during the other six months.

Notes / Birthdays

This nostalgic pavilion, which is overgrown with colourful roses in summer, is turned into a mysterious backdrop by fog and hoar frost.
Design: Piet Oudolf (NL)

December

2 December

It's now time for a few last jobs at the garden pond. Withered plant matter, fish excrement and other organic substances in the water lead to decomposition processes. If there's a closed ice layer, however, the resulting gases cannot escape – putting the inhabitants of the pond at risk. This is why you should put an ice preventer into place before the pond freezes up. This floats on the surface of the water and keeps it partially ice-free, which is sufficient to ensure gas exchange and oxygen supply. At the edge of the pond, shorten the herbaceous plants as you see fit. Reeds in the shallow water zone should stay where they are, however. This is because their hollow blades allow gas exchange even if there's a closed layer of ice on the pond.

Notes / Birthdays

In winter, too, moisture-loving plants such as hydrangeas, grasses and sturdy shrubs assume the charming role of a mediator between the trees and the garden pond.
Garden and design: Peter Janke (D)

December

3 December

Black frost is the most stressful aspect of winter for plants. While temperatures beneath a blanket of snow don't drop below 0°C, when there is no snow the frost can penetrate deep into the unprotected soil and block off the water supply to the plants. If the situation is aggravated by wind and sun, evergreen plants and plants with shallow roots can easily dry up. Before this happens, you should protect shrubs with spruce brushwood, straw mats or upended boxes. Trees and shrubs can be protected from the worst by a layer of leaves or bark mulch. Evergreen trees and shrubs are given additional shade through the use of jute, reed mats or fleece to reduce evaporation.

Notes / Birthdays

This shrub protection from nature for nature consists of huge gunnera leaves. To prevent the wind from blowing them away, weigh them down with pieces of the stalk of this mammoth plant.

December

4 December

Twigs cut today, on Saint Barbara's Day, can surprise you with fresh blossoms at Christmas time. If they've already caught the frost a few times by then, putting them in a warm room will fool them into thinking it's spring and that temperatures are rising. The reason: the period from 4 to 24 December corresponds precisely with the time when the cherry trees traditionally used for this purpose open their blossoms. Other plants which flower in an enchanting way include Farrer's viburnum, flowering almond, ornamental plum tree, hydrangea and ornamental blackcurrant. Cut into the twigs at an angle and leave them in water in a cool place for a few days.

To trigger the impulse to flower, put them into a bath full of lukewarm water before arranging them indoors.

Notes / Birthdays

Flowering quinces (*Chaenomeles,* right) and sloes are also suitable for use as St Barbara twigs. To ensure that they blossom, you should choose shoots with plump buds if possible.

December

5 December

Advent can become a long festival of joy if the view of garden and terrace from the window is festive-looking. It's no wonder that we perceive red and green indoor and outdoor decorations as a joyful promise in the dark weeks leading up to Christmas. We can only surmise why these became the classic colours of Advent and Christmas. In this less colourful season, we encounter green, the colour of nature, in the evergreen twigs of deciduous trees and conifers. For many of us, it no doubt symbolises the hope for spring, growth and immortality. By contrast, red – the colour of blood, life and love – symbolises joy, strength and fire.

Notes / Birthdays

There's no doubt that the joy of anticipation is able to thrive here. Asied from frost-hardy accessories as outdoor decorations, the fine gardening implements also make appropriate Christmas gifts for gardeners.

Garden and design: Peter Janke (D)

December

6 December

Nobody will want to design a garden based entirely on what looks nice in winter. However, as long as you ensure a balanced alternation of summergreen and evergreen silhouettes of trees and shrubs when choosing plants, you can create exquisite garden spaces. If you supplement these large-scale structures with sturdy shrubs displaying different growth forms, the garden will turn into a winter paradise when covered in frost and snow. In regions with a lot of snow, the choice of plants is more restricted, for filigree grasses cannot withstand heavy masses of snow for very long.

Notes / Birthdays

Shrubs can present themselves in the herbaceous border with seed buttons and umbrellas, puffed out, chaotic or bolt upright. If you want to be creative with their shapes in winter, you'll often find what you're looking for among the wild species and varieties, many of which are sturdy in winter.

Garden: Anja and Piet Oudolf, design: Piet Oudolf (NL)

December

7 December

In regions with a lot of snow, even extremely sturdy trees and shrubs are endangered by avalanches coming off protruding roofs. Once you realise that a cubic metre of powdery snow weighs about 100 kg, that same quantity of hard-packed snow weighs twice as much, while avalanche snow can even weigh up to 800 kg per cubic metre, it's clear why plants need protection.

You can ensure their survival with a stable wooden roof resting on solid posts to catch the falling snow. To allow thawing moisture to run off well, position the roof at an angle so that the water is directed away from the plants.

Notes / Birthdays

Although tone-in-tone, this shrub ensemble is far from boring. Against the upright backdrop of grasses, coneflower *(Echinacea)* and gay feather *(Liatris)* display their distinctive seed pods all winter long.
Design: Piet Oudolf (NL)

December

8 December

Even when it's cold and inhospitable outside, the slogan for friends of gardens and nature is now "keep your eyes open!", because this is the time when the season reveals its climatological magic. As soon as the temperature drops below 0°C, atmospheric humidity and fog turn into small ice crystals and cover all surfaces in a fine coating of rime.

By contrast, the long needles and plumes of hoar frost don't form until there's an atmospheric humidity of more than 90 per cent, below-zero temperatures of –8°C and a light wind. This blows the ice crystals onto fences, branches etc., where they then build up.

This is why plumes of hoar frost always grow towards the wind. The more the air cools and the longer this takes, the larger the resulting ice needles.

Notes / Birthdays

The Arkansas false aster *(Vernonia arkansana/crinita* 'Mammuth') is a late developer. It's 2 metres high and blooms in a luminous reddish-violet from September to October. It fascinates with its icy beauty all through the winter.

December

9 December

Trellis hedges have the advantage that they stay the same size and don't get out of hand. The only parts that get thicker with the years are the trunks and the shoots. Many deciduous trees and shrubs are suitable for shaping in this way, but the most popular of them all is the common lime *(Tilia × europaea* 'Pallida'), which tolerates all kinds of soils. The trees are available pre-cultivated in a variety of sizes and trunk heights. The latter determine the dimensions of the trellis required. As soon as the trees have shed their foliage, remove all twigs from the trunk and main branches. In the case of freshly planted lime trees, leave twig stumps on the side branches during the first two years. This makes them sprout better and thicken more rapidly.

Notes / Birthdays

The common lime tree *(Tilia × europaea* 'Pallida') in winter trellis hedges looks as if it's wearing mittens. The thickened parts are the result of being cut back. The main shoots will come out of them in spring.
Garden: De Wiersse (NL)

December

10 December

When nature falls into its great sleep, the colours of life – red, orange and yellow – largely disappear. This doesn't mean the garden has to sink into depression, however. The subtle use of just two types of tree is enough to fill it with colours and shapes. Warm reddish-brown and green are available all winter long – for example in the leaves of the common beech *(Fagus sylvatica)* and the oak, which stay on the tree for a long time, and in evergreen trees and shrubs. Moreover, green sculptures of box or yew and columns or cones consisting of conifers stand out wonderfully against a backdrop of beech hedges. On the other hand, evergreen hedges made of yew, thuja, juniper or false cypress form a picturesque background for beeches or oaks.

Notes / Birthdays

The shape and colour of a line of conifers in the form of plump columns loosens up the regularity of this beech hedge.
Garden: De Wiersse (NL)

December

11 December

The garden scene on the right with its frost-free elements shows that the patterns of garden design don't just consist of optical rules but are based on human experience and allow emotional phenomena to be perceived by the senses. The line of sight and the pathway both lead from the dark to the light. The beech arbour thus conveys the comforting truth that bad days are soon followed by light and bright ones. The pathway has a similar symbolic function, promising comfort, good company and protection in the pavilion to those who walk down it. But not immediately, however, for the way is also the goal. Here, a small circular flower bed, in which a putto on a column enriches the ensemble with a playful height element, invites you to pause for a moment's thought.

Notes / Birthdays

Consistency of form in spite of the changing seasons characterises this beech bower, which turns a fresh pastel green in spring and gives shade in summer, with brown leaves following in autumn and winter.
Garden: De Wiersse (NL)

December

12 December

Hydrangea blossoms sparkle with hoar frost as if crowned with lace. Unfortunately, snow often puts an end to their splendour. On the other hand, it provides excellent protection against the cold for this shallow-rooted plant, whose resistance to frost varies depending on the species and variety.

- In cold regions, all freshly planted hydrangeas are given a mulch layer made of leaves and brushwood inserted in the ground at an angle to protect the base shoots.
- Later, paniculate hydrangeas *(Hydrangea paniculata)* and North American wild hydrangeas *(Hydrangea arborescens,* for example the well-known 'Annabelle' variety) no longer require any protection.
- Big-leaf hydrangeas and lacecap hydrangeas *(Hydrangea macrophylla)* show varying degrees of frost-hardiness depending on the variety. In very cold places, therefore, it's preferable to grow them frost-free in tubs.

Notes / Birthdays

Hydrangeas thrive delightfully in the shelter of a large tree and backed up by rhododendrons. However, snow can push the shoots apart and snap them if they aren't tied together or the blossoms aren't cut off in time.
Garden: Elisabeth Imig and Silke Imig-Gerold (D)

December

13 December

When you decorate gate and doors, hallway and rooms, walls and mantelpiece, windows and table for the most joyous festival of the year, you shouldn't forget to include terrace and conservatory. Frost-proof table arrangements, garlands and floral arrangements made of natural materials such as cones, twigs, roots, seed pods and the last leaves shine in a wintry festiveness refined by the frost or in an artificial glitter look from a spray can. Baubles, candles and stars can add some brightly coloured anticipation to the proceedings. Cosy lamplight makes up for the early dusk. LED technology in the form of twinkling stars or strings of lights allows you to illuminate trees and shrubs safely outside the window too.

Notes / Birthdays

Summer has left its last traces behind in this arrangement of pumpkins, ornamental apples and evergreens. The light of lanterns and candles livens up the snowy idyll.
Garden: Elisabeth Imig and Silke Imig-Gerold (D)

December

14 December

The appearance of your garden in winter benefits if you're familiar with plants which have unusual infructescences, for example the blue bean–like fruits of the blue bean shrub *(Decaisnea fargesii)* or the pencil-like seed vessels of the Indian bean tree *(Catalpa bignonioides)*. Conifer cones also make an attractive winter decoration. Cones of fir trees *(Abies)* aren't suitable for decorations, though, as they decompose when they fall. The cones of *Abies balsamea* 'Piccolo', *Abies lasiocarpa* 'Compacta' and *Abies koreana* are of great decorative value when still on the tree. However, if you're looking for cones that keep longer for making decorations, you'll find them around spruces *(Picea)*, pines *(Pinus)*, larches *(Larix)*, Douglas firs *(Pseudotsuga)* and cedars *(Cedrus)*.

Notes / Birthdays

The cone-type infructescences of the stag's horn sumach *(Rhus typhina)* stay on the tree all winter long. Before that, the attractive little tree delights us with its breathtaking autumn colouring. As it tends to form runners, it should always be planted with a root barrier.

December

15 December

The purple berries of the beautyberry *(Callicarpa bodinieri* 'Profusion') seem almost outlandish and are noticeable from a distance. The shrub is only 2–3 metres high, and its loosely branched growth makes it suitable for small gardens too.

Its only demands are for chalk-free soil, a place in the sun and good winter protection in cold regions. In July/August, it bears small purple blossoms in cymes, which in turn produce shiny purple berries in September/October. These will stay on the tree throughout the winter. In addition, the leaves turn to orange-yellow. The shrub is not only a feast for the eyes – it's also very popular among bees and bumble-bees, and birds feed on it too.

Notes / Birthdays

The poisonous berries of the beautyberry *(Callicarpa bodinieri* 'Profusion'), which seem almost artificial and resemble coloured beads, bring exotic colours into the garden.

December

16 December

In some years, the leaves of roses which usually shed their greenery stay on the plant all winter. This can frequently be observed in the case of shrub roses in particular. Two causes are usually responsible for this. Firstly, these rose leaves stay healthy until late autumn as a result of careful maintenance and balanced fertilisation, and so they don't fall off prematurely. Secondly, winter doesn't come on gently but with a sudden cold snap. When this happens, the natural ripening process of the foliage is skipped and the leaves die while still on the shrub. If these "frozen" leaves are healthy, you should leave them on the rose, for they protect the shoots from frost, wind and sun.

Notes / Birthdays

Hoar frost has transformed the leaves and hips of the hedgerow rose *(Rosa rugosa)* into candied sweets. After being affected by frost in this way, however, the fruits become soft and pulpy and are no longer edible.

December

17 December

Sea buckthorn is one of the most wind–resistant shrubs of all, and it proves this by occurring with particular frequency in sandy, gravelly coastal regions. Its deep and widespread root system is even able to anchor it in the loosely packed soils it prefers.

Before winter and snowstorms shake high trees and maybe even fell them, the time when they are without leaves provides a good opportunity to check their stability and their condition, that is to say, find out whether roots or trunk have rotten places. This is recommended because responsibility for any damage caused by a fallen tree lies with the owner of the tree. Gardeners or tree experts can help here.

The yellowish-red to orange-red fruits of sea buckthorn *(Hippophae rhamnoides)* are to be found on the shoots of female plants between long thorns. After the leaves are shed, they remain clearly visible and persist all winter long, but are then no longer of any use to human beings and are inedible.

December

18 December

Ornamental apples are little multi-talents. After they've blossomed profusely in April/May, a rich fruit set in yellow to red appears. With some varieties, this stays on the tree until winter is in progress. These varieties include 'Butterball' (yellow), 'Evereste' (orange-red), 'Prof. Sprenger' (orange-yellow), 'Red Jade' (red), 'Red Sentinel' (dark red) and 'Wintergold' (yellow). The hard little fruits range in size from that of cherries to that of walnuts, and they're much sought after during Advent, when they are often used in wreaths, floral arrangements and garlands.

Tip: if you fix your arrangements in place using floral foam, you should wrap wire mesh tightly around it beforehand so that it doesn't break apart under the weight of the materials.

Notes / Birthdays

The orange-red fruits of the ornamental apple 'Evereste' reach a size of up to 2.5 cm, stay on the tree until early December and usually retain their fresh red colour even after frost. Its profusion of blossoms and pollen also makes 'Evereste' a popular pollinator variety.

December

19 December

The arrangement you see on the right shows an effect that can be used for small gardens too: the distinctive contrast between summer-green and evergreen plants and between free-growing and topiarised shrubs. In terms of bioclimatic architecture, yews retain a consistent geometrical appearance throughout the year, allowing the deciduous trees and shrubs in the background to display the change of the seasons all the more distinctly.

Tip: if the garden isn't designed as a completely formal one, hedges or walls integrated as scenery always seem more agreeable if they don't finish with a hard outline but taper off in a curve (or in steps).

This scenery covered with hoar frost looks as if it came out of a construction kit. Here, the mythical yew *(Taxus baccata)* proves that it's one of the evergreens with the greatest tolerance to being cut back.
Garden: De Wiersse (NL)

December

20 December

Anything that can withstand the cold is highly valued from now until spring, for it can be used to decorate and liven up the terrace, balcony and garden even in the most inhospitable period of the year. Besides the classic objects made of stone and metal, busts, figures, columns and vessels made of hardy frost-resistant stoneware or plastics are becoming increasingly popular. During Advent, these are joined by frost-proof Christmas accessories such as strings of fairy lights, stars, angels, hearts, Christmas-tree baubles, garlands, lanterns and decorative objects from nature such as cones, moss objects, attractive shoots and mistletoe.

If there really is a white Christmas, Jack Frost can easily include the festive flower arrangements in his wintry magic.

Notes / Birthdays

Reindeer in the garden must mean that Father Christmas is on his way. The metal stickers with their golden coating underline the friendly charm of the holly (*Ilex aquifolium* 'Aurea Marginata') and its yellow edging.

Garden and design: Peter Janke (D)

December

21 December

Every self-respecting gardener has "his" tools which he would never trade in because there's nothing better around. Nevertheless, there are countless Christmas presents which would be welcomed by gardeners. Just think of the large number of magnificent rose poles, plant supports, obelisks and trellises. Or think of the apparatuses designed for special plants, be they roses, vegetables or pond plants – not to mention the handy gloves, gardening aprons, knee cushions, baskets or skin-care products for chapped gardener's hands. Presents of this type selected with love don't just give joy at Christmas, but during the entire gardening year.

Notes / Birthdays

The trappings of a real passion for gardening reveal that there are criteria other than the latest fashion trends and chic originality.

December

22 December

With its shiny evergreen leaves and signal red berries, common holly *(Ilex aquifolium)* displays the classic colours of Christmas. As foliage and fruits stay fresh on the branches for a long time even in warm rooms, they're a popular Christmas decoration, not only in the United Kingdom.

If you want your holly to bear a lot of fruit, you'll need a female variety and a male pollinator for pollination (such as *Ilex meserveae* 'Blue Prince'). If there isn't much room, choose the self-fertile 'J.C. van Tol' variety, which bears a lot of berries even without a partner. Caution: holly leaves and berries are highly toxic!

Notes / Birthdays

The leaf form of holly changes with age, as does that of ivy. The thorny toothed foliage then acquires smooth edges. Like all varieties of holly, the yellow-edged variety 'Aurea Marginata' is takes easily to being cut back. However, trimming it into shape is usually done at the expense of the berries.

December

23 December

To ensure that the pre-cultivation of the biennial flowers wasn't carried out in vain, they should be protected at this point. The biennials sown out in July, such as foxgloves *(Digitalis)*, mullein *(Verbascum)*, dame's violet *(Hesperis matronalis)*, forget-me-nots *(Myosotis sylvatica)*, pansies *(Viola × wittrockiana)*, sweet William *(Dianthus barbatus)* or Canterbury bells *(Campanula medium)* were planted at the intended place in a bed or herbaceous border in late summer. To ensure that they survive the winter and flower reliably in the following year, give them some loose winter protection. Stick brushwood into the ground over the plants at an angle so that they aren't crushed or suffocated below it.

Notes / Birthdays

In mixed herbaceous borders, biennial young plants find protection from sun and wind between box spheres, grasses and shrubs. When there's no protective covering, the frost can still penetrate deep into the area around the roots.
Garden and design: Peter Janke (D)

December

24 December

Roses only rarely flower at Christmas in our latitudes. The Christmas tree is therefore a much more reliable symbol of hope and new life. If the tree is to shed as few needles as possible, don't choose a spruce, and test the tree for freshness before you buy it: the cut surface must be light-coloured and the needles shouldn't fall off when you bend them back. Remove the net immediately after transport. Then cut off a piece of the trunk to open the channels and store the tree in a bucket of water in a cool, shady, frost-free place. Once indoors, place the Christmas tree away from the heating and be sure to supply it regularly with water and freshness retainer.

Notes / Birthdays

"Lo, How a Rose E'er Blooming" is the title of an old Christmas carol. In the garden, this is usually not the case. However, bought roses can be integrated into Christmas decorations too.

December

25 December

Gardens have their highlights in all seasons when useful things are presented in a way that creates atmosphere. For example, it's worthwhile decorating wrapped rose stems in a festive way; livening up a covered shrub bed with coloured baubles; adorning rose arches with apples and fat balls for birds; and illuminating stars or iron obelisks with strings of fairy lights. If a potted Christmas tree complete with roots is later to be moved to the garden, it shouldn't stay in the warm house for longer than ten days. Water it every two days and store it in a shady place indoors before use. It can then be planted out from March onwards.

Notes / Birthdays

This pavilion in a snow-covered garden is festively adorned with a green wreath and red ribbon and contributes to the feeling of Christmas.
Garden and design: Peter Janke (D)

December

26 December

In regions with a lot of snow, you should take special measures to prevent it from bending or breaking certain trees and shrubs.

- To ensure that snow doesn't snap tall narrow conifers, push them apart or deform them, wrap wide tape around them in loose spirals.
- Keep large spheres, columns, cones and other sculptures cut from evergreen trees and shrubs in shape by wrapping tape around them.
- The shoots of berry bushes, overhanging shrub roses and other ornamental shrubs with soft shoots should be tied loosely around a pole driven into the ground to ensure that they aren't pushed apart.

Notes / Birthdays

The thick downy covering of snow on the garden chairs may look inviting and encourage you to go out and get some fresh air, but strong snowfalls can soon become a problem for trees and shrubs.
Garden and design: Peter Janke (D)

December

27 December

Now is a good time for felling trees. However, it isn't always worth doing away with an old tree "root and branch". There are alternatives which reduce the effort required and offer new creative possibilities.

- If you leave 30–40 cm of the base standing, it can be overgrown spherically by ivy. Adding one to two box spheres to it will create an evergreen ensemble.
- If you cut the trunk at a height of 70-100 cm, it forms a stand for a bird-bath, a table or a decorative object.
- If a large part of the trunk (including twig implants) stays standing, *Clematis montana* or a rambler rose can climb around it.

Snow also covers the evergreen leaves of the Oregon grape *(Mahonia* x *media* 'Winter Sun', right), which opens its light yellow flower clusters as early as January. This frost-sensitive shrub needs protection from sun and frost in cold regions.
Garden and design: Peter Janke (D)

December

28 December

The days between 24 December and 6 January are especially quiet and dark. Little wonder, then, if this did give rise to the notion that the boundary between this world and the beyond was more permeable than usual during these twelve nights. As a result, many customs aimed at warding off evil spirits developed, as did blessing rituals for the New Year. One thing which should become a ritual for gardeners in this period is the examination of the tub plants in their winter domicile. Remove shed leaves and water the plants extremely moderately. Check them for pests, for the plants are weakened and sensitive at this time. If they turn out to be afflicted, remedy this immediately.

Notes / Birthdays

This yew sofa is reminiscent of the throne of an ice princess. Frost-resistant and covered with a velvety cushion, it defies the winter.
Garden: De Kempenhof (NL)

December

29 December

Even roses include groups which require neither heaped-up soil nor brushwood protection
in places with a raw climate. These include the
following plants:

• Domestic and European wild roses. If some
  shoots are frozen off, the roses will replace
  the missing parts quickly by sprouting out at
  the base again.
• Small shrub roses (ground cover roses). These
  are extremely frost-resistant and can survive
  the winter without the protection described
  here.
• Many of the annual shrub roses and old roses
  (especially Gallica and Alba roses). These
  usually survive the winter quite well.

Tip: in regions with a lot of snow, you should
just tie varieties with soft shoots together and
stabilise them using a pole.

Notes / Birthdays

A deep calm also descends on snowy natural
gardens when birds and crickets go silent and
pond and stream gradually turn to ice.
Garden and design: Peter Janke (D)

December

30 December

Freshly planted young fruit trees must be given adequate protection for the winter. Their wood is still soft, making them more sensitive to frost than older trees. Also, they don't yet have a thick bark to protect them against cold close to the ground. Young apple and cherry trees in particular are most at risk.

In addition, freshly planted trees and shrubs haven't yet developed an extensive root system to supply them with sufficient moisture. This is why we protect young trees with a mulch covering against ground frost and simultaneously with reed or bamboo mats to safeguard against evaporation, overheating and browsing by game. These are fixed around the trunk from the ground up to where the crown branches off.

Two evergreen cypresses (*Cupressus sempervirens* 'Pyramidalis') form the entrance to this avenue of old apple trees. Like pointing fingers, they draw attention to the fact that a special corridor begins here.
Garden and design: Peter Janke (D)

December

31 December

New Year's Eve can be celebrated in a number of different ways. Outdoor New Year's Eve parties on the terrace with radiant heaters, home-made snow bars and hot food and drink from barbecue, soup terrine and punch-bowl are becoming increasingly popular.

On this day, however, plant lovers can also indulge their passion and give the occasion a special flavour with purchased flowers. Hanging amaryllis flowers are an unusual decorative idea. Fix a bamboo frame above the table and suspend the exquisite long-stemmed blossoms from it. In this way, you can look them "in the eye" at table. If you pour additional water into their hollow stalks, they'll stay fresh for weeks.

Notes / Birthdays

To make this elegant table decoration, just lay out a strip of turf or moss on a film. Then arrange candlesticks, tea lights, white irises and ivy vines on it.

Garden and design: Son Muda Gardens, Majorca (E)

December

January Contents

February Contents

March Contents

April Contents

May Contents

June Contents

July Contents

August Contents

September Contents

October Contents

November Contents

December Contents

© Justyna Kryzanowska

After graduating in humanities and literary studies, **Gisela Keil** combined her intimate attachment to gardens with her love of books. As a lector and packager, she initiated and produced some of the most successful long-selling and best-selling books of gardening tips for various well-known publishers. A professional of the book business, she started writing herself 20 years ago. She soon became known as a freelance journalist and writer of garden books, authoring a number of successful books and magazine articles.

After completing his studies at the Düsseldorf Academy of Art, **Jürgen Becker** dedicated his work to architectural, interior and travel photography. Since the 1990s, he has focused on the subject of gardens, becoming one of the most successful and best-known photographers in this field worldwide. His photographs appear in renowned international magazines, books and calendars and he has received a number of important international awards.
Jürgen Becker lives and works as a publisher and photographer in Hilden, near Düsseldorf.

Acknowledgements
The photographer and the author would like to thank the programme director of the DVA, Dr. Thomas Hagen, for his idea to publish this book and for the great commitment with which he has supported its production. Their heartfelt thanks also go to all garden owners and designers who opened the gates to their private and exclusively designed garden realms. The resulting images not only invite you to daydream, but also provide a treasure trove of inspiration for all concerned.

The following country abbreviations were used when identifying the gardens and garden designers (at the end of the captions in each case): AUS = Australia; B = Belgium; CH = Switzerland; D = Germany; E = Spain; GB = Great Britain; LUX = Luxembourg; NL = Netherlands; S = Sweden; USA = United Stated of America